Getting started with Google Guava

Write better, more efficient Java, and have fun doing so!

Bill Bejeck

[PACKT] open source*
PUBLISHING   community experience distilled

BIRMINGHAM - MUMBAI

Getting started with Google Guava

First published: August 2013

Production Reference: 1080813

Published by Packt Publishing Ltd.
Livery Place
35 Livery Street
Birmingham B3 2PB, UK.

ISBN 978-1-78328-015-5

www.packtpub.com

Cover Image by Suresh Mogre (suresh.mogre.99@gmail.com)

Credits

Author
Bill Bejeck

Reviewers
John Drum

David Sletten

Acquisition Editor
Usha Iyer

Commissioning Editor
Poonam Jain

Technical Editors
Nitee Shetty

Aniruddha Vanage

Copy Editors
Gladson Monterio

Insiya Morbiwala

Aditya Nair

Alfida Paiva

Laxmi Subramanian

Project Coordinator
Esha Thakker

Proofreader
Mario Cecere

Indexer
Monica Ajmera Mehta

Production Coordinator
Nitesh Thakur

Cover Work
Nitesh Thakur

About the Author

Bill Bejeck is a senior software engineer with 10 years experience across a wide range of projects. Currently he is working on the storage and analysis of financial data using Hadoop. He has a B.A in Economics from the University of Maryland and an M.S in Information Systems from Johns Hopkins University. Bill also enjoys blogging at `http://codingjunkie.net`.

I would like to thank my wife Beth for her support, encouragement, and patience, making my work on this book possible (not to mention making life easy for me overall!), and my children Allison, Emily, and Brady for their unconditional love and support, and the joy they bring to my life every day.

About the Reviewers

John Drum is a bicoastal software engineer with over 20 years of experience in industries ranging from e-commerce to financial services.

David Sletten is a software engineer at Near Infinity in Northern Virginia. He probably would have learned quite a few things from the author if Bill had not left the company.

www.PacktPub.com

Support files, eBooks, discount offers and more

You might want to visit www.PacktPub.com for support files and downloads related to your book.

Did you know that Packt offers eBook versions of every book published, with PDF and ePub files available? You can upgrade to the eBook version at www.PacktPub.com and as a print book customer, you are entitled to a discount on the eBook copy. Get in touch with us at service@packtpub.com for more details.

At www.PacktPub.com, you can also read a collection of free technical articles, sign up for a range of free newsletters and receive exclusive discounts and offers on Packt books and eBooks.

http://PacktLib.PacktPub.com

Do you need instant solutions to your IT questions? PacktLib is Packt's online digital book library. Here, you can access, read and search across Packt's entire library of books.

Why Subscribe?

- Fully searchable across every book published by Packt
- Copy and paste, print and bookmark content
- On demand and accessible via web browser

Free Access for Packt account holders

If you have an account with Packt at www.PacktPub.com, you can use this to access PacktLib today and view nine entirely free books. Simply use your login credentials for immediate access.

Table of Contents

Preface	**1**
Chapter 1: Getting Started	**5**
Introducing Google Guava	**5**
The case for using Guava	**6**
What is this book about?	**6**
Installing Guava	**7**
Using Guava with Maven or Gradle	**7**
Getting the source code for the book	8
Summary	**10**
Chapter 2: Basic Guava Utilities	**11**
Using the Joiner class	12
Time for a review	14
Using the Splitter class	14
Time for a review	16
Working with strings in Guava	16
Using the Charsets class	17
Using the Strings class	18
Using the CharMatcher class	19
Using the Preconditions class	20
Object utilities	22
Getting help with the toString method	22
Checking for null values	23
Generating hash codes	23
Implementing CompareTo	24
Summary	**25**

Chapter 3: Functional Programming with Guava	**27**
Using the Function interface	**28**
Guidelines for using the Function interface	29
Using the Functions class	**29**
Using the Functions.forMap method	30
Using the Functions.compose method	30
Using the Predicate interface	**32**
An example of the Predicate interface	32
Using the Predicates class	**33**
Using the Predicates.and method	33
Using the Predicates.or method	34
Using the Predicates.not method	34
Using the Predicates.compose method	34
Using the Supplier interface	**35**
An example of the Supplier interface	35
Using the Suppliers class	**36**
Using the Suppliers.memoize method	37
Using the Suppliers.memoizeWithExpiration method	37
Summary	**38**
Chapter 4: Working with Collections	**39**
The FluentIterable class	**40**
Using the FluentIterable.filter method	40
Using the FluentIterable.transform method	41
Lists	**42**
Using the Lists.partition method	42
Sets	**42**
Using the Sets.difference method	43
Using the Sets.symmetricDifference method	43
Using the Sets.intersection method	43
Using the Sets.union method	44
Maps	**44**
Using the Maps.uniqueIndex method	45
Using the Maps.asMap method	45
Transforming maps	46
Multimaps	**46**
ArrayListMultimap	46
HashMultimap	48
BiMap	**49**
Using the BiMap.forcePut method	49
Using the BiMap.inverse method	50

Table **50**
Table operations 51
Table views 52
Range **52**
Ranges with arbitrary comparable objects 53
Immutable collections **54**
Creating immutable collection instances 54
Ordering **55**
Creating an Ordering instance 55
Reverse sorting 55
Accounting for null 56
Secondary sorting 56
Retrieving minimum and maximum values 57
Summary **58**
Chapter 5: Concurrency **59**
Synchronizing threads **60**
Monitor **61**
Monitor explained 62
Monitor best practice 62
Different Monitor access methods 62
ListenableFuture **63**
Obtaining a ListenableFuture interface 64
FutureCallback **65**
Using the FutureCallback 65
SettableFuture **66**
AsyncFunction **67**
FutureFallback **68**
Futures **69**
Asynchronous Transforms 69
Applying FutureFallbacks 69
RateLimiter **70**
Summary **71**
Chapter 6: Guava Cache **73**
MapMaker **74**
Guava caches **74**
Cache 74
LoadingCache 76
Loading values 76
Refreshing values in the cache 76
CacheBuilder **77**
CacheBuilderSpec **79**

CacheLoader	**81**
CacheStats	**81**
RemovalListener	**82**
RemovalNotification	82
RemovalListeners	83
Summary	**84**
Chapter 7: The EventBus Class	**85**
EventBus	**86**
Creating an EventBus instance	86
Subscribing to events	86
Posting the events	87
Defining handler methods	87
Concurrency	87
Subscribe – An example	**87**
Event Publishing – An example	**89**
Finer-grained subscribing	**90**
Unsubscribing to events	**93**
AsyncEventBus	**94**
Creating an AsyncEventBus instance	94
DeadEvents	**94**
Dependency injection	**95**
Summary	**96**
Chapter 8: Working with Files	**97**
Copying a file	**98**
Moving/renaming a File	**98**
Working with files as strings	**98**
Hashing a file	**100**
Writing to files	**101**
Writing and appending	101
InputSupplier and OutputSupplier	**102**
Sources and Sinks	102
ByteSource	**103**
ByteSink	**103**
Copying from a ByteSource class to a ByteSink class	**104**
ByteStreams and CharStreams	**104**
Limiting the size of InputStreams	105
Joining CharStreams	105
Closer	**107**
BaseEncoding	**108**
Summary	**109**

Chapter 9: Odds and Ends   111

  Creating proper hash functions   111

    Checksum hash functions   112

    General hash functions   112

    Cryptographic hash functions   113

  BloomFilter   113

    BloomFilter in a nutshell   113

    Funnels and PrimitiveSinks   114

    Creating a BloomFilter instance   114

  Optional   116

    Creating an Optional instance   117

  Throwables   118

    Getting the chain of Throwables   118

    Obtaining the Root Cause Throwable   119

  Summary   120

Index   121

Preface

Java continues to maintain its popularity, and is one of the main languages used in the software industry today. One of the strengths of Java is the rich ecosystem of libraries available for developers, helping them to be more productive. Guava is a great example of such a library that will give Java developers a boost in their productivity. In addition, as we start to use Guava, we'll get ideas that we can start implementing in our own code.

What this book covers

Chapter 1, *Getting Started* introduces Guava, and in addition to that, makes the case for using Guava.

Chapter 2, *Basic Guava Utilities* covers basic functionality for working with strings and objects.

Chapter 3, *Functional Programming with Guava* introduces the functional programming idioms provided by Guava.

Chapter 4, *Working with Collections* covers the collection utilities and classes that enhance the existing Java collections.

Chapter 5, *Concurrency* shows how using Guava's concurrency abstractions help us to write better concurrent code.

Chapter 6, *Guava Cache* introduces Guava caching, including a self-loading cache.

Chapter 7, *The EventBus Class* covers how we can use the Guava EventBus class for event-based programming.

Chapter 8, Working with Files shows how Guava greatly simplifies reading and writing of files, especially for those using Java 6.

Chapter 9, Odds and Ends wraps up our coverage of Guava including the Optional class for avoiding nulls, Guava hashing functionality, and the BloomFilter data structure.

What you need for this book

You will need to have Java 1.6 or greater installed. Additionally, you will need to have Maven or Gradle installed to pull in the dependencies required to work with the available sample code.

Who this book is for

This book is for Java developers; there is no minimum level of experience required. There is something for everyone who works with Java, from the beginner to the expert programmer.

Conventions

In this book, you will find a number of styles of text that distinguish between different kinds of information. Here are some examples of these styles, and an explanation of their meaning.

Code words in text are shown as follows: "The Function interface gives us the ability to incorporate functional programming into Java and greatly simplify our code."

A block of code is set as follows:

```
<dependency>
    <groupId>com.google.guava</groupId>
    <artifactId>guava</artifactId>
    <version>14.0</version>
</dependency>
```

When we wish to draw your attention to a particular part of a code block, the relevant lines or items are set in bold:

```
dependencies {
    compile group: 'com.google.guava' name: 'guava' version: '14.0'
}
```

New terms and important words are shown in bold. Words that you see on the screen, in menus or dialog boxes for example, appear in the text like this: "clicking the **Next** button moves you to the next screen".

> Warnings or important notes appear in a box like this.

> Tips and tricks appear like this.

Reader feedback

Feedback from our readers is always welcome. Let us know what you think about this book—what you liked or may have disliked. Reader feedback is important for us to develop titles that you really get the most out of.

To send us general feedback, simply send an e-mail to feedback@packtpub.com, and mention the book title via the subject of your message.

If there is a topic that you have expertise in and you are interested in either writing or contributing to a book, see our author guide on www.packtpub.com/authors.

Customer support

Now that you are the proud owner of a Packt book, we have a number of things to help you to get the most from your purchase.

Downloading the example code

You can download the example code files for all Packt books you have purchased from your account at http://www.packtpub.com. If you purchased this book elsewhere, you can visit http://www.packtpub.com/support and register to have the files e-mailed directly to you.

Errata

Although we have taken every care to ensure the accuracy of our content, mistakes do happen. If you find a mistake in one of our books — maybe a mistake in the text or the code — we would be grateful if you would report this to us. By doing so, you can save other readers from frustration and help us improve subsequent versions of this book. If you find any errata, please report them by visiting http://www.packtpub. com/submit-errata, selecting your book, clicking on the **errata submission form** link, and entering the details of your errata. Once your errata are verified, your submission will be accepted and the errata will be uploaded on our website, or added to any list of existing errata, under the Errata section of that title. Any existing errata can be viewed by selecting your title from http://www.packtpub.com/support.

Piracy

Piracy of copyright material on the Internet is an ongoing problem across all media. At Packt, we take the protection of our copyright and licenses very seriously. If you come across any illegal copies of our works, in any form, on the Internet, please provide us with the location address or website name immediately so that we can pursue a remedy.

Please contact us at copyright@packtpub.com with a link to the suspected pirated material.

We appreciate your help in protecting our authors, and our ability to bring you valuable content.

Questions

You can contact us at questions@packtpub.com if you are having a problem with any aspect of the book, and we will do our best to address it.

1
Getting Started

In this chapter, we are going to cover a little bit on Guava's history. Then, we are going to make a case on why you should use a well-established library instead of "rolling your own". We are going to talk about where you can get the Guava library and how to install it and finally, how to set up the source code that comes with this book.

Introducing Google Guava

What is Google Guava? Starting out originally in 2007 as the "Google Collections Library", which provided utilities for working with Java collections, the Google Guava project has evolved into being an essential toolkit for developers working in Java. There is something for everyone in Guava. There are classes for working with strings, collections, concurrency, I/O, and reflection. The Function interface gives us the ability to incorporate functional programming into Java and greatly simplify our code. The Supplier interface helps with creational patterns. But Guava is more than just abstractions that take some of the boilerplate out of Java, or convenience methods that we all feel should have been in Java to begin with. It's about writing a good code and making it more resilient and concise. So my suggestion is to not just use Guava, but look at the source code and get a feel of how things are done. Then try to apply the same principles you've learned to your own code. Finally, have fun!

The case for using Guava

As software developers, we like to think we can do it all. We instinctively want to write our own libraries for handling things we see on a day-to-day basis. Of course, we think the code we've written is bullet proof, and we know why we've written unit tests, and they all pass! Well, I have some bad news for you, we all are not as smart as we'd like to be. Actually, it's really not about how smart you are. It's more about writing code that's not only unit tested, but is also being used by a large group of developers and having their input weigh in on the code. Guava is used by hundreds of production applications, and as of July 2012, there were a staggering 286,000 individual unit tests in the guava-tests package. So when it comes down to it, you are far better off using a library such as Guava, than rolling your own. Besides, according to *Larry Wall* (the author of Perl), one of the best qualities of a software engineer is laziness, not in the "I don't want to work" way but in the "Why reinvent the wheel when this works so well" way. Really good developers will look for an established library to help with a problem before starting to write their own.

What is this book about?

Our goal for the book is that it will always sit next to your computer while you are coding. When you come across a situation where you need to know how to use something from Guava, or what Guava has that could solve your problem, our hope is that this book will have the answer, and if not, at least point you in the right direction. This book will have source code for every topic covered. Most of the time, the source code will be in the form of unit tests. Sometimes, coming up with meaningful examples can be difficult, and a unit test will quickly show how the code is supposed to work. Also, having unit tests will be invaluable as Guava tends to have a frequent release schedule, and running the tests will give you a quick indication if anything has changed from the previous release. While it will be impossible to cover every part of the Guava library, we've tried to make the book comprehensive and cover most of what we think a typical developer will find useful. Finally, we hope that the book will be as easy to read and enjoyable as it is useful.

Installing Guava

To start working with Guava, all you need to have is Java 1.6 or a higher version installed. The version of Guava covered in this book is 14, which is the latest as of this writing. The following are the steps you need to perform to get started with Guava:

1. Guava can be downloaded directly by navigating to `https://code.google.com/p/guava-libraries/` and clicking on the **guava-14.jar** link.

2. If you are working with GWT and would like to take advantage of Guava in your code, there is also a GWT compatible version that can be downloaded by clicking on the **guava-gwt-14.jar** link on the same page. A separate version for GWT is required because everything in the standard Guava distribution will not be compiled to JavaScript by the GWT compiler.

3. Once the JAR file is downloaded, add it as an external library to your IDE (IntelliJ, NetBeans, or Eclipse). If you are working with a text editor (Sublime Text 2 or TextMate), add the JAR file to your classpath.

4. The API docs for Guava can be found at `http://docs.guava-libraries.googlecode.com/git-history/release/javadoc/index.html`.

You are now ready to start working with Guava.

Using Guava with Maven or Gradle

It's possible to use Guava with build tools such as Maven or Gradle.

To use Guava in your Maven projects, add the following to the dependencies section of your `pom.xml` file:

```xml
<dependency>
    <groupId>com.google.guava</groupId>
    <artifactId>guava</artifactId>
    <version>14.0</version>
</dependency>
```

If you are using Gradle, first add the Maven Central Repository (if you haven't already) by adding the following to your `build.gradle` file:

```
repositories {
    mavenCentral()
}
```

Then, add the following highlighted section to the dependencies section of the `build.gradle` file:

```
dependencies {
    compile group: 'com.google.guava' name: 'guava' version: '14.0'
}
```

For more information on Maven, go to `http://maven.apache.org/`, and for more information on Gradle, go to `http://www.gradle.org/`.

It's important to mention that Guava has only one dependency, JSR-305.

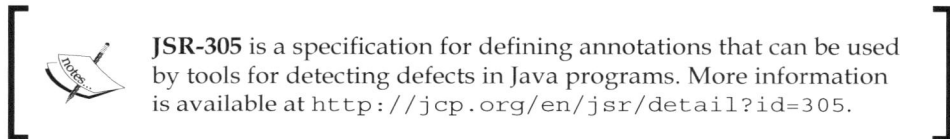

> **JSR-305** is a specification for defining annotations that can be used by tools for detecting defects in Java programs. More information is available at `http://jcp.org/en/jsr/detail?id=305`.

If you are not planning on using the JSR-305 JAR directly, you don't need to include it with your dependencies. But if you are going to use JSR-305, you will need to explicitly define that dependency, as it is not going to be pulled in automatically. Also, if you plan to use Guava from within Scala, you will have to include the JSR-305 JAR file. While the Java compiler does not require the library containing the annotations when compiling, the Scala compiler currently does. While this may change in the future, for now, if you want to use Guava with Scala, you will need to have the JSR-305 JAR file in your classpath as well.

Getting the source code for the book

The source code for the book is structured as a Java project, with a structure consistent with that of either a Gradle or Maven project. As mentioned earlier, most of the source code will be in the form of unit tests. If you don't have either Gradle or Maven installed, I strongly recommend that you install one of them, as it makes running the unit tests easy and will pull down Guava and all the dependencies for the project.

The following are the steps for obtaining and working with the source code from the book:

1. Download the source code from `http://www.packtpub.com/support`.
2. Extract the zipped source file to a location on your computer.
3. Change the directory to `guava-book-code` directory.
4. If you have Gradle installed, run `gradle install`.
5. If you have Maven installed, run `mvn install`.

After following these steps, you will have Guava installed as well as the dependencies needed for the source code from the book. If all went well, you should have seen a bunch of unit tests being executed and they should have all passed. I strongly recommend using either of the build tools previously mentioned, with the source code. This will make it very easy to change the versions of Guava as it evolves and runs the tests for the book's source code and see if anything has changed. If you don't have either of the build tools installed, you will need to download the following dependencies to run all the examples listed in the book:

- Lucene v4.2: `http://lucene.apache.org/`
- Spring Java config Version 3.2: `http://www.springsource.org/spring-framework`
- H2 (embedded database) v1.3.170: `http://www.h2database.com/html/main.html`
- JUnit v4.11: `https://github.com/junit-team/junit/wiki/Download-and-Install`

The source code for the book was written on a MacBook Pro v10.7.5, using Java 7, the Gradle build system, and the IntelliJ IDE.

Downloading the example code

You can download the example code files for all Packt books that you have purchased from your account at `http://www.packtpub.com`. If you purchased this book elsewhere, you can visit `http://www.packtpub.com/support` and register to have the files e-mailed directly to you.

Summary

So far we've gone over a brief history of Guava, and how it can improve the quality of your code as well as make your job a little easier, if not more fun. We also saw the importance of using well-tested and widely used libraries instead of rolling your own. Finally, we went over where to get Guava from, how to install it, and how to get the source code for the book. In the next chapter, we begin our exploration of Google Guava by covering the basic utility classes found in the `com.google.common.base` package along with the `ComparisonChain` class from the `the com.google.common.collect` package.

2
Basic Guava Utilities

In the previous chapter, we talked about what Guava is and how to install it. In this chapter we will start using Guava. We are going to demonstrate the basic functionalities provided by Guava and how it can help with some of the common everyday tasks encountered in programming.

In this chapter we will be covering:

- The use of the `Joiner` class to concatenate strings together with a specified delimiter. We will also cover the `MapJoiner` class that performs the same operation on the key value pairs of a map.
- The use of the `Splitter` class, which is the logical inverse of the `Joiner` class. Given a string and a delimiter, the `Splitter` class will produce substrings broken out by the provided delimiter.
- Working with strings; specifically, how to perform common operations such as removing parts of a string, matching strings, and more using the `CharMatcher` and `Strings` classes.
- The `Preconditions` class, which provides methods for asserting certain conditions you expect variables, arguments, or methods to adhere to.
- Some basic utilities for working with any Java object, including help with the `toString` and `hashCode` methods and an easier way of implementing the `Comparable` interface.

Using the Joiner class

Taking arbitrary strings and concatenating them together with some delimiter token is something that most programmers deal with on a regular basis. It usually involves taking an array, list, or an iterable and looping over the contents, appending each item to a StringBuilder class, and appending the delimiter afterwards. This tends to be a cumbersome process and will typically look as follows:

```
public String buildString(List<String> stringList, String delimiter){
        StringBuilder builder = new StringBuilder();
        for (String s : stringList) {
            if(s !=null){
                builder.append(s).append(delimiter);
            }
        }
        builder.setLength(builder.length() - delimiter.length());
        return builder.toString();
}
```

Note the need to remove the last delimiter that was appended to the very end of the string. Not very complicated, but it's still some boilerplate code that can be more easily handled by using the Joiner class. Here's the same example from earlier (assuming the use of " | " as the delimiter character), but using a Joiner class:

```
Joiner.on("|").skipNulls().join(stringList);
```

This is much more concise and there's no chance of making an error in formatting the string. If you wanted to add a replacement for null values instead, you would use the following:

```
Joiner.on("|").useForNull("no value").join(stringList);
```

There are a few points we need to emphasize here about using the Joiner class. The Joiner class is not restricted to working only with strings. One could pass in an array, iterable, or varargs of any object. The result is built by calling Object.toString() for each element that was passed in. As a consequence, if the skipNulls or useForNull method is not used, a NullPointerException error will be thrown. Once created, a Joiner class is immutable, and therefore thread-safe, and can be used as a static final variable. With that in mind, consider the following code snippet:

```
Joiner stringJoiner = Joiner.on("|").skipNulls();
    //the useForNull() method returns a new instance
    of the Joiner!
    stringJoiner.useForNull("missing");
        stringJoiner.join("foo","bar",null);
```

In the preceding code example, the useForNull() method call will have no effect on the original Joiner class and null values will still be omitted from the result string.

The Joiner class not only returns strings but also has methods that can work with the StringBuilder class:

```
StringBuilder stringBuilder = new StringBuilder();
Joiner joiner = Joiner.on("|").skipNulls();
//returns the StringBuilder instance with the values foo,bar,baz
 appeneded with "|" delimiters
 joiner.appendTo(stringBuilder,"foo","bar","baz")
```

In the preceding example, we are passing a StringBuilder instance to the Joiner class and the StringBuilder object is returned.

The Joiner class can be used with classes that implement the Appendable interface.

```
FileWriter fileWriter = new FileWriter(new File("path")):
 List<Date> dateList = getDates();
 Joiner joiner = Joiner.on("#").useForNulls(" ");
 //returns the FileWriter instance with the values
   appended into it
 joiner.appendTo(fileWriter,dateList);
```

Here we see a similar example. We are passing in a FileWriter instance and a list of Date objects to the Joiner class. The Joiner class will append the joined list of dates to the FileWriter instance and then return the FileWriter instance.

As we can see, Joiner is a very useful class that makes a common task very easy to deal with. There is a special method to cover before we move on—the MapJoiner method. The MapJoiner method works in the same way as the Joiner class but it joins the given strings as key value pairs with a specified delimiter. A MapJoiner method is created as follows:

```
mapJoiner = Joiner.on("#").withKeyValueSeparator("=");
```

Let's quickly review what is going on here:

- The Joiner.on("#") call is creating a Joiner object
- The Joiner object is created in the call to the on method and calls the withKeyValueSeparator method, which takes the calling Joiner instance to construct a MapJoiner object that is returned by the method call

Here is a unit test demonstrating the use of the MapJoiner method (my apologies for the obvious American Football reference, NFC East Division to be specific):

```
@Test
    public void testMapJoiner() {
        //Using LinkedHashMap so that the original
          order is preserved
        String expectedString = "Washington D.C=Redskins#New York
        City=Giants#Philadelphia=Eagles#Dallas=Cowboys";
        Map<String,String> testMap = Maps.newLinkedHashMap();
        testMap.put("Washington D.C","Redskins");
        testMap.put("New York City","Giants");
        testMap.put("Philadelphia","Eagles");
        testMap.put("Dallas","Cowboys");
        String returnedString = Joiner.on("#").
        withKeyValueSeparator("=").join(testMap);
        assertThat(returnedString,is(expectedString));
    }
```

Time for a review

The preceding unit test is creating a LinkedHashMap instance with string keys and values. It's worth noting that we are using the static factory method newLinkedHashMap(), which is found in the Maps class in the com.google.common. collect package. Then, the Joiner class is used to create a string by joining the key value pairs together. Finally, we assert that the string returned by the Joiner operation matches the expected string value. Also note the use of the Hamcrest matcher method, is(), that is bundled with JUnit.

Using the Splitter class

Another common task for programmers is to take a string with some delimiter character and split that string on the delimiter and obtain an array of the parts of the string. If you need to read in text files, you do this all the time. But the behavior of the String.split method leaves something to be desired, as evidenced by the following example:

```
String testString = "Monday,Tuesday,,Thursday,Friday,,";
   //parts is [Monday, Tuesday, , Thursday,Friday]
   String[] parts = testString.split(",");
```

As you can see, the `String.split` method truncated the last two entries in the concatenated string. In some cases, that might be the behavior you want, but that is something that should be left to the programmer and should not happen by default. The `Splitter` class helps with this situation. The `Splitter` class performs the inverse of the functions of the `Joiner` class. A `Splitter` class can split on a single character, a fixed string, a `java.util.regex.Pattern` package, a string representing a regular expression, or a `CharMatcher` class (another Guava class, which will be covered in this chapter as well). A `Splitter` instance is created by calling the `on` method and specifying the separator to be used. Once you have the `Splitter` instance, you will call the `split` method, which returns an iterable object containing the individual string parts from the source.

```
Splitter.on('|').split("foo|bar|baz");

Splitter splitter = Splitter.on("\\d+");
```

In the preceding examples, we see a `Splitter` instance using a `'|'` character and another `Splitter` instance using a regular expression pattern that would split on one or more consecutive digits embedded in a string.

The `Splitter` class also has an option for dealing with any leading or trailing whitespace in the `trimResults` method.

```
//Splits on '|' and removes any leading or trailing whitespace
Splitter splitter = Splitter.on('|').trimResults();
```

Just like the `Joiner` class, `Splitter` is immutable on creation, so care must be taken to not call the `trimResults` method after creating the original `Splitter` class; for example:

```
Splitter splitter = Splitter.on('|');
//Next call returns a new instance, does not
modify the original!
splitter.trimResults();
//Result would still contain empty elements
Iterable<String> parts = splitter.split("1|2|3|||");
```

The `Splitter` class, like `Joiner` with its accompanying `MapJoiner` class, has a `MapSplitter` class. The `MapSplitter` class can take a string in which the keys and values are delimited with one value and the key value pair is delimited with another value and returns a `Map` instance with the entries in the same order as the given string. Constructing a `MapSplitter` class is done as follows:

```
//MapSplitter is defined as an inner class of Splitter
Splitter.MapSplitter mapSplitter =    Splitter.on("#").
withKeyValueSeparator("=");
```

As we can see, the MapSplitter class is created in the same way as the MapJoiner class. First we specify the base Splitter object to use and then specify the delimiter that the MapSplitter class is to use to separate out the key value pairs. The following is an example of the MapSplitter class, which is the inverse of our example of the MapJoiner class:

```
@Test
    public void testSplitter() {
        String startString = "Washington D.C=Redskins#New York
        City=Giants#Philadelphia=Eagles#Dallas=Cowboys";
        Map<String,String> testMap = Maps.newLinkedHashMap();
        testMap.put("Washington D.C","Redskins");
        testMap.put("New York City","Giants");
        testMap.put("Philadelphia","Eagles");
        testMap.put("Dallas","Cowboys");
        Splitter.MapSplitter mapSplitter =
        Splitter.on("#").withKeyValueSeparator("=");
        Map<String,String> splitMap =
        mapSplitter.split(startSring);
    assertThat(testMap,is(splitMap));
      }
```

Time for a review

The preceding unit test takes a string and uses the MapSplitter class to create a LinkedHashMap instance. Then we assert that the Map instance created by the MapSplitter class matches our expectations.

This wraps up our coverage of Joiners and Splitters, two classes that should be in every Java developer's toolbox.

Working with strings in Guava

Regardless of the language you prefer to use, all programmers work with strings and it can sometimes be tedious and error prone. At some point, we all need to read data from a file or database table and reformat the data, either for presentation to users or for storing in a format that suits our requirements. Fortunately, Guava provides us with some very useful classes that can make working with strings much easier. These classes are:

- CharMatcher
- Charsets
- Strings

Now let's take a look at how we can use these in our code.

In the first example, the unit test that we are demonstrating uses the `Ascii` class method for determining if a character is in lower case. The second example is a demonstration of converting a string from lowercase to uppercase.

Using the Charsets class

In Java, there are six standard character sets that are supported on every Java platform. This is relevant because it's not uncommon to have the need to run the following code:

```
byte[] bytes = someString.getBytes();
```

But there is a problem with the preceding statement. By not specifying the character set that you want the bytes returned in, you will get the default of the system running the code, which could lead to problems if the default character set on the system is not the one you are expecting to deal with. It's considered best practice to obtain the underlying bytes of a string in the following manner:

```
try{
    bytes = "foobarbaz".getBytes("UTF-8");
}catch (UnsupportedEncodingException e){
    //This really can't happen UTF-8 must be supported
}
```

But there are still two problems with this example:

- UTF-8 must be supported on the Java platform, so in reality the `UnsupportedEncodingException` error will never be thrown
- Since we are using a string to specify the character set definition, we could make a spelling mistake, which would cause an exception to be thrown

This is where the `Charsets` class helps. The `Charsets` class provides static final references to the six character sets supported on the Java platform. Using the `Charsets` class, we can transform the earlier example to the following:

```
byte[] bytes2 = "foobarbaz".getBytes(Charsets.UTF_8);
```

It's worth noting that as of Java 7, there is a `StandardCharsets` class that also provides static final definitions to the six standard character sets supported on the Java platform. Now let's move on to the `Strings` class.

Using the Strings class

The `Strings` class provides a few handy utility methods for working with strings. Have you ever had to write something like the following?

```
StringBuilder builder = new StringBuilder("foo");
char c = 'x';
for(int i=0; i<3; i++){
  builder.append(c);
 }
return builder.toString();
```

The previous example, which spans 6 lines of code, can now be replaced with one line.

```
Strings.padEnd("foo",6,'x');
```

What's important to note here is that the second argument, `6`, specifies the minimum length of the returned string and not how many times to append the `x` character to the original string. If the provided string already had a length of 6 or greater, no padding would occur. There is also a corresponding `padStart` method with the same signature and behavior with the exception that the character is inserted in front of the given string until the minimum length is met.

There are three very useful methods in the `Strings` class that are meant specifically for dealing with possible null values:

- `nullToEmpty`: This method takes a string as an argument and returns the original string if the value is not null or has a length greater than 0, otherwise it returns `""`
- `emptyToNull`: This method performs in a manner similar to `nullToEmpty`, but will return a null value if the string parameter is null or is an empty string
- `isNullOrEmpty`: This method performs a null and length check on the string argument and returns `true` if the string is in fact null or empty (length of `0`)

It would probably be a good idea to always use the `nullToEmpty` method on any string objects passed as arguments.

Using the CharMatcher class

The `CharMatcher` class provides functionality for working with characters based on the presence or absence of a type of character or a range of characters. The methods in the `CharMatcher` class make formatting and working with text very simple. For example, here's how you take a string that spans multiple lines and format it to be on one line with a space where the line break was previously present:

```
CharMatcher.BREAKING_WHITESPACE.replaceFrom(stringWithLinebreaks,' ');
```

There is also a version of `replaceFrom` that takes a `CharSequence` value as the replacement value instead of a single character.

To remove multiple tabs and spaces (multiple meaning consecutive) and collapse them into single spaces, use the following code:

```
@Test
    public void testRemoveWhiteSpace(){
        String tabsAndSpaces = "String  with      spaces      and
            tabs";
        String expected = "String with spaces and tabs";
        String scrubbed = CharMatcher.WHITESPACE.
        collapseFrom(tabsAndSpaces,' ');
        assertThat(scrubbed,is(expected));
    }
```

In the preceding test, we are taking a string with multiple spaces and tabs and replacing all of them with a single space, all in one line of code.

The previous example works in some cases, but what if the string in question had spaces at the beginning that we also wanted to remove? The returned string will have a space in the front, but that is easily handled by using the `trimAndCollapseFrom` method:

```
@Test
    public void testTrimRemoveWhiteSpace(){
        String tabsAndSpaces = "    String  with      spaces      and
            tabs";
        String expected = "String with spaces and tabs";
        String scrubbed = CharMatcher.WHITESPACE.
        trimAndCollapseFrom(tabsAndSpaces,' ');
        assertThat(scrubbed,is(expected));
    }
```

In this test, we are again taking a string with leading spaces as well as multiple spaces and tabs and removing the leading spaces and collapsing the multiple consecutive spaces into one space each, again in one line!

While listing all of the methods available in the CharMatcher class would be impractical, here is an example where instead of replacing a group of matching characters, we retain the characters that match:

```
@Test
 public void testRetainFrom(){
     String lettersAndNumbers = ""foo989yxbar234"";
     String expected = ""989234"";
     String retained = CharMatcher.JAVA_DIGIT.
     retainFrom(lettersAndNumbers);
     assertThat(expected,is(retained));
 }
```

In this example, we are taking the string ""foo989yxbar234"" and retaining all digits found in the string.

Before moving on, we should talk about one final powerful feature of the CharMatcher class: the ability to combine CharMatcher classes to create a new CharMatcher class. For example let's say you want to create a matcher for numbers or whitespace:

```
CharMatcher cm = CharMatcher.JAVA_DIGIT.or(CharMatcher.WHITESPACE);
```

This will now match any number (as defined by the definition of a digit in Java) or a whitespace character.

The CharMatcher class is powerful and is very useful when it comes to working with strings in Java.

Using the Preconditions class

The Preconditions class is a collection of static methods used to verify the state of our code. Preconditions are very important because they guarantee our expectations for successful code execution are met. If the conditions are different from what we expect, we get instant feedback about where the problem is. As before, using preconditions are important for ensuring the behavior of our code and are very useful in debugging.

You can certainly write your own preconditions, like so:

```
if(someObj == null){
   throw new IllegalArgumentException(" someObj must
   not be null");
}
```

By using preconditions (with static imports), our check for a null parameter is more concise.

```
checkNotNull(someObj,"someObj must not be null");
```

Next, we are going to show the usage of preconditions with a highly contrived example:

```
public class PreconditionExample {
    private String label;
    private int[] values = new int[5];
    private int currentIndex;

    public PreconditionExample(String label) {
        //returns value of object if not null
        this.label = checkNotNull(label,"Label can''t be null");
    }

    public void updateCurrentIndexValue(int index, int valueToSet) {
        //Check index valid first
        this.currentIndex = checkElementIndex(index, values.length,
"Index out of bounds for values");
        //Validate valueToSet
        checkArgument(valueToSet <= 100,"Value can't be more than
100");
        values[this.currentIndex] = valueToSet;
    }

    public void doOperation(){
        checkState(validateObjectState(),"Can't perform operation");
    }

    private boolean validateObjectState(){
        return this.label.equalsIgnoreCase("open") && values[this.
currentIndex]==10;
    }

}
```

The following is a summary of the four methods from the previous example:

- checkNotNull (T object, Object message): This method returns the object if it is not null; otherwise a NullPointerException error is thrown.

- checkElementIndex (int index, int size, Object message): In this method, the value of the index variable is the position of the element you are trying to access and the value of the size variable is the length of the array, list, or string. The index variable is retuned if valid; otherwise an IndexOutOfBoundsException error is thrown.

- checkArgument (Boolean expression, Object message): This method evaluates a Boolean expression involving the state of a variable passed to a method. The Boolean expression is expected to evaluate to true, otherwise an IllegalArgumentException error is thrown.

- checkState (Boolean expression, Object message): This method evaluates a Boolean expression involving the state of the object, not the arguments. Again, the Boolean expression is expected to evaluate to true, otherwise an IllegalArgumentException error is thrown.

Object utilities

In this section we are going to cover the utility methods that help with checking for null values and assist in creating toString and hashCode methods. We are then going to take a look at a helpful class that takes the pain out of implementing the Comparable interface.

Getting help with the toString method

While the toString method is essential when it comes to debugging, writing one is tedious. However, the Objects class makes use of the toStringHelper method, which makes this task much easier. Consider the following simple class and take a look at the toString() method that follows:

```
public class Book implements Comparable<Book> {

    private Person author;
    private String title;
    private String publisher;
    private String isbn;
     private double price;
....
```

```
public String toString() {
    return Objects.toStringHelper(this)
            .omitNullValues()
            .add("title", title)
            .add("author", author)
            .add("publisher", publisher)
            .add("price",price)
            .add("isbn", isbn).toString();
}
```

Let's explore what's going on in the toString method:

- First we are passing a reference of the Book class in the call that creates an instance of Objects.ToStringHelper
- The second method call, omitNullValues, will exclude any null property values from being added
- Each call to add provides a label and the property to include in the string representation of the Book object.

Checking for null values

The firstNonNull method takes two arguments and returns the argument that is not null.

```
String value = Objects.firstNonNull(someString,""default value"");
```

The firstNonNull method can be used as a way of providing a default value when you are not sure if an object is null. A word of caution though: if both arguments are null, a NullPointerException error will be thrown.

Generating hash codes

Writing the hashCode method for an object is essential, but tedious. The Objects class makes use of the hashCode method, which can make this process easier. Consider a Book class having four fields: title, author, publisher, and isbn. The following code shows how you can use the Object.hashCode method:

```
public int hashCode() {
    return Objects.hashCode(title, author, publisher, isbn);
}
```

Implementing CompareTo

Again, using our Book class, the following is a typical implementation of the compareTo method:

```
public int compareTo(Book o) {
        int result = this.title.compareTo(o.getTitle());
        if (result != 0) {
            return result;
        }

        result = this.author.compareTo(o.getAuthor());
        if (result != 0) {
            return result;
        }

        result = this.publisher.compareTo(o.getPublisher());
        if(result !=0 ) {
            return result;
        }

        return this.isbn.compareTo(o.getIsbn());
    }
```

Now let's take a look at the implementation of compareTo using the ComparisonChain class:

```
public int compareTo(Book o) {
        return ComparisonChain.start()
                .compare(this.title, o.getTitle())
                .compare(this.author, o.getAuthor())
                .compare(this.publisher, o.getPublisher())
                .compare(this.isbn, o.getIsbn())
                .compare(this.price, o.getPrice())
                .result();
    }
```

The second example is much more compact and is also easier to read. Also, the ComparisonChain class will stop making comparisons with the first non-zero result, the only way a zero will be returned is if all comparisons result in a zero.

Summary

We have covered a lot of ground in this chapter. We learned how Guava makes life easier when working with delimited strings using Joiner, Splitter, and the very useful MapJoiner and MapSplitter classes. We also learned about Guava's ability to work with strings using the Charsets, CharMatcher, and Strings classes.

We saw how to make our code more robust and improve debugging with the use of the Preconditions class. In the Objects class, we learned about some useful methods to help with setting default values and creating toString and hashCode methods. We also saw how to use the ComparisonChain class to make implementing the compareTo method easier.

In the next chapter, we take a look at how we can use Guava to leverage some functional programming in our code, by using the Function and Predicate interface that, when used sparingly, can add power and clarity to our programs.

3
Functional Programming with Guava

In this chapter, we start to notice that using Guava has an impact on how we write our code and makes development easier. We will take a look at how using certain Guava interfaces and classes can help us, by applying well-established patterns to make our code more maintainable as well as robust.

Specifically, we will be covering the following topics in this chapter:

- The `Function` interface: This explains how we can introduce functional programming to our Java programs. It also explains how best we can use the `Function` interface and recognize where its usage is not appropriate

- The `Functions` class: This class is a collection of static methods that are used to work with implementations of the `Function` interface

- The `Predicate` interface: This is an interface that evaluates a given object for certain criteria and returns true if the object has met the criteria

- The `Predicates` class: This is a companion class to the `Predicate` interface that has static utility methods for working with implementations of the `Predicate` interface

- The `Supplier` interface: This is an interface used to supply an object of a given type. We will see how to use the `Supplier` interface to implement a variety of patterns to create objects

- The `Suppliers` class: This is a class that provides some default implementations of the `Supplier` interface

Using the Function interface

Functional programming emphasizes the use of functions to achieve its objectives versus changing state. This is in contrast with imperative programming that typically relies on the changing state and is the approach that is familiar with most of the developers. The Function interface from Guava gives us the ability to introduce some functional programming into our Java code.

The Function interface contains only two methods:

```
public interface Function<F,T> {
    T apply(F input);
    boolean equals(Object object);
}
```

We won't go into much detail on the equals method other than to say that if Object A equals Object B, the result of calling apply on A should equal the result of calling apply on B. The apply method simply takes an input object and returns an output object. A good Function implementation should have no side effects, meaning the object passed as an argument should remain unchanged after the apply method has been called. Here's an example that takes an instance of a java.util.Date object and returns a formatted string representing the date:

```
public class DateFormatFunction implements Function<Date,String> {

@Override
public String apply(Date input) {
    SimpleDateFormat dateFormat = new SimpleDateFormat("dd/mm/yyyy");
        return dateFormat.format(input);
    }
}
```

In this first example, we can clearly see that a java.util.Date object is being transformed using a SimpleDateFormat class to give us a string representation of the date in our desired format. While this example is probably overly simplistic, it demonstrates the purpose of the Function interface, transforming an object while hiding the implementation details. Although in this example we are using a class that implements the Function interface, we could have easily defined Function inline as an anonymous class. Consider the following example:

```
Function<Date,String> function = new Function<Date, String>() {
        @Override
    public String apply( Date input) {
            return new
SimpleDateFormat("dd/mm/yyyy").format(input);
            }
        };
```

There is no difference between the previous two examples; one is simply a class that implements the Function interface and the other is an anonymous class. One advantage to having a class implement the Function interface is that you could use dependency injection to pass a Function interface into a collaborating class and increase your code's cohesion.

Guidelines for using the Function interface

This is probably a good time to discuss introducing the Function interface into your code and for anonymous class usage. With Java in its current state, we don't have closures as they exist in other languages. While the release of Java 8 will change this, for now Java's answer to closures is to use anonymous classes. While an anonymous class functions effectively in the same way as a closure, the syntax can be bulky and when used too much, can make your code harder to follow and maintain. As a matter of fact, when we analyze the previous example, while it serves its purpose for demonstrating how Functions works, we don't gain much from using it. For example, consider the more typical, imperative approach to achieving the same goal:

```
public String formatDate(Date input) {
        return new SimpleDateFormat("dd/mm/yyyy").format(input);
    }
```

Now compare the previous example of the anonymous class implementing the Function interface. This final example is much easier to read. When to use Function comes down to where you need to perform your transformations. If you have a class with a Date instance field and a method that returns the Date instance in an expected String format, you are probably better off implementing that method as demonstrated in the latter example. However, if you have a collection of Date objects and need to obtain a list containing the string representations of those dates, the Function interface could be a better approach. The main point here is that you shouldn't start throwing anonymous Function instances throughout your code simply because you can. Take a look at your code; have you really gained from using a functional approach? We will see several examples of using the Function interface when we cover Guava Collections in *Chapter 4, Working with Collections*, and caches in *Chapter 6, Guava Cache*.

Using the Functions class

The Functions class contains a handful of useful methods for working with Function instances. In this section, we will cover how two of these useful methods can help make the Function interface even more productive.

Using the Functions.forMap method

The `forMap` method takes `Map<K,V>` and returns a function (`Function<K,V>`) whose `apply` method will perform a map lookup. For example, consider the following class representing a state in the United States:

```
public class State {

    private String name;
    private String code;
    private Set<City> mainCities = new HashSet<City>();


}
```

Now consider that you have a map named `stateMap` in the form of `Map<String,State>` where the string key would be the state abbreviation. Now to create the function that would perform the lookup by state code, you would simply do the following:

```
Function<String,State> lookup = Functions.forMap(stateMap);
//Would return State object for NewYork
lookup.apply("NY");
```

There is one caveat to using the `Functions.forMap` method. The map returned by `Functions.forMap` will throw an `IllegalArgumentException` exception if the given key is not found in the map. However, there is another version of `Functions.forMap` that takes an additional parameter to be used as a default value, should the given key not be found in the map. By using a `Function` interface to perform the state lookups, you can easily change out the implementation. When combining it with a `Splitter` object to create a map or when using some of the other methods for map creation in the Guava collection package, we are leveraging the power of Guava in our code.

Using the Functions.compose method

Now assume you have another class representing a city, which is shown as follows:

```
public class City {

    private String name;
    private String zipCode;
    private int population;
```

```
    public String toString() {
        return name;
    }
}
```

Consider the following scenario: you would like to create a Function instance that, given a State object, would be transformed into comma-separated String of the major cities in that state. The Function object would look as follows:

```
public class StateToCityString implements Function<State,String> {

    @Override
    public String apply(State input) {
        return Joiner.on(",").join(input.getMainCities());
    }
}
```

Now let's take this a step further. You would like to have a single Function instance that takes the abbreviation for a state and returns comma-separated String of the top cities for that state. Guava provides a great solution to this situation. It's the Functions.compose method that takes two Function instances as arguments and returns a single Function instance that is a composition of the two. So we can take an example of our previous two Function instances and perform the following:

```
Function<String,State> lookup = Functions.forMap(stateMap);
Function<State, String> stateFunction = new StateToCityString();
Function<String,String> composed =
Functions.compose(stateFunction ,lookup);
```

Now a call to composed.apply("NY") would return the following:

```
"Albany,Buffalo,NewYorkCity"
```

Let's take a minute to walk through the order of method calls here. composed Function takes the NY parameter and calls lookup.apply(). The return value from the lookup.apply() method is used as a parameter to stateFunction. apply(). Finally, the result of the stateFunction.apply() method is returned to the caller. Without the use of our composed function, the previous example would look as follows:

```
String cities = stateFunction.apply(lookup.apply("NY"));
```

Using the Predicate interface

The Predicate interface is a functional *cousin* to the Function interface. Like the Function interface, the Predicate interface has two methods. Here's the interface's definition:

```
public interface Predicate<T> {
  boolean apply(T input)
  boolean equals(Object object)
}
```

As was the case with the Function interface, we won't be going into detail about the equals method here either. The apply method returns the result of applying Predicate to the input. Where the Function interface is used to transform objects, the Predicate interface is used to filter objects. The usage guidelines for Predicates are the same as the guidelines for Functions; don't use Predicates when a simpler procedural approach will suffice. Also, a Predicate function should not have any side effects. In the next chapter, where we cover Collections, we will see how to make the best use of the Predicate interface.

An example of the Predicate interface

Here is a simple example of a Predicate interface that will use the City class from the recent example. Here we will define a Predicate to determine if a city has minimum population:

```
public class PopulationPredicate implements Predicate<City> {

    @Override
    public boolean apply(City input) {
        return input.getPopulation() <= 500000;
    }
}
```

In this example, we are simply checking the population field for the City object and returning true if the population is less than or equal to 500000. Typically, you would see a Predicate interface such as this defined as an anonymous class and used as a filter condition for placing elements in a collection. Since the Predicate interface is so similar to the Function interface, much of what we stated for the Function interface applies to the Predicate interface too.

Using the Predicates class

The `Predicates` class is a collection of useful methods for working with `Predicate` instances. The `Predicates` class offers some very helpful methods that should be expected from working with Boolean conditions, chaining `Predicate` instances with "and" or "or" conditions, and providing a "not" that evaluates to true if the given `Predicate` instance evaluates to false and vice versa. There is also a `Predicates.` `compose` method, but it takes a `Predicate` instance and a `Function` object and returns `Predicate` that evaluates the output from the given `Function` object. Let's take a look at some examples so we can get a better understanding of how we can use `Predicates` in our code. Before we move on to look at specific examples, let's assume we have the following two instances of `Predicates` classes defined (in addition to `PopulationPredicate` defined previously) for our `City` object:

```
public class TemperateClimatePredicate implements Predicate<City> {

    @Override
    public boolean apply(City input) {
        return input.getClimate().equals(Climate.TEMPERATE);
    }
}


public class LowRainfallPredicate implements Predicate<City> {

    @Override
    public boolean apply(City input) {
        return input.getAverageRainfall() < 45.7;
    }
}
```

It bears repeating, while not required, that we typically would define `Predicate` instances as anonymous classes, but for clarity we will be using concrete classes.

Using the Predicates.and method

The `Predicates.and` method takes multiple `Predicate` instances and returns a single `Predicate` instance that will return true if all the component `Predicate` instances evaluate to true (consistent with the logical AND operator). If any of the component `Predicate` instances return false, the evaluation of any other `Predicate` instances is stopped. For example, let's say we wanted to only accept cities with a population of under 500,000 and having average rainfall of less than 45.7 inches per year:

```
Predicate smallAndDry =
Predicates.and(smallPopulationPredicate,lowRainFallPredicate);
```

There is also an option to call `Predicates.and` with the following signatures:

```
Predicates.and(Iterable<Predicate<T>> predicates);
Predicates.and(Predicate<T> ...predicates);
```

Using the Predicates.or method

The `Predicates.or` method takes multiple `Predicates` and returns a single `Predicate` instance that returns true if any of the component `Predicate` instances evaluate to true (consistent with the logical OR operator). Once a component `Predicate` instance returns true, no further evaluations are made. For this example, let's assume we want to include cities with a population of less than or equal to 500,000 or having a temperate climate:

```
Predicate smallTemperate =
Predicates.or(smallPopulationPredicate,temperateClimatePredicate);
```

`Predicates.or` has the same overloaded method signatures like the `Predicates.and` method:

```
Predicates.or(Iterable<Predicate<T>> predicates);
Predicates.or(Predicate<T> ...predicates);
```

Using the Predicates.not method

The `Predicates.not` method takes a Predicate object and performs a logical negation of the component Predicate. Suppose we want to find cities with populations of over 500,000. Instead of having to write another `Predicate`, we can use `Predicate.not` on our existing `PopulationPredicate` object:

```
Predicate largeCityPredicate =
Predicate.not(smallPopulationPredicate);
```

Using the Predicates.compose method

The `Predicates.compose` method takes `Function` and `Predicate` as arguments and evaluates the given `Predicate` instance on the output returned from `Function`. In the following example, we are going to introduce a new `Predicate`:

```
public class SouthwestOrMidwestRegionPredicate implements
Predicate<State> {

    @Override
    public boolean apply(State input) {
```

```
        return input.getRegion().equals(Region.MIDWEST) ||
                input.getRegion().equals(Region.SOUTHWEST);
    }
}
```

Next, we are going to re-use state lookup `Function` to create a Predicate that will evaluate whether the state returned from our function is located in either the midwest or the southwest:

```
Predicate<String> predicate =
Predicates.compose(southwestOrMidwestRegionPredicate,lookup);
```

Using the Supplier interface

The `Supplier` interface is an interface with one method and is shown as follows:

```
public interface Supplier<T> {
    T get();
}
```

The `get` method returns an instance of type `T` and only of that type. The `Supplier` interface helps us implement several of the typical creational patterns. When `get` is called, we could always return the same instance (singleton) or a new instance with each invocation. A `Supplier` interface also gives you the flexibility to use lazy instantiation by not constructing an instance until the `get` method is called. Also, since the `Supplier` is an interface, unit testing becomes much easier, as compared to other approaches for creating objects such as a static factory method. In short, the power of the `Supplier` interface is that it abstracts the complexity and details of how an object needs to be created, leaving the developer free to create an object in whatever way he/she feels is the best approach. Let's take a look at how we might use a `Supplier` interface.

An example of the Supplier interface

The following code is an example of the `Supplier` interface:

```
public class ComposedPredicateSupplier implements
Supplier<Predicate<String>> {

    @Override
    public Predicate<String> get() {
        City city = new City("Austin,TX","12345",250000, Climate.SUB_
TROPICAL,45.3);
```

```
        State state = new State("Texas","TX", Sets.newHashSet(city),
Region.SOUTHWEST);
        City city1 = new City("New York,NY","12345",2000000,Climate.
TEMPERATE,48.7);
        State state1 = new State("New York","NY",Sets.
newHashSet(city1),Region.NORTHEAST);
        Map<String,State> stateMap = Maps.newHashMap();
        stateMap.put(state.getCode(),state);
        stateMap.put(state1.getCode(),state1);
        Function<String,State> mf = Functions.forMap(stateMap);
        return Predicates.compose(new RegionPredicate(), mf);
    }
}
```

In this example, we can see that we are using `Functions.forMap` to create a
`Function` instance that looks up a state in the United States by its abbreviation, and
then uses a `Predicate` instance to evaluate which region in the country the state is
found in. Then we are using the `Function` and `Predicate` instances as arguments
to the `Predicates.compose` method whose result is returned by a call to the `get`
method. We also used two static factory methods, `Maps.newHashMap()` and `Sets.
newHashSet()`, both of which are Guava utility classes found in the `com.google.
common.collect` package and which will be covered in the next chapter. Note that
here we are choosing to return a new instance each time. We could have just as easily
done all of this work in the constructor of the `ComposedPredicateSuplier` class
and returned the same instance with each call to `get`, but as we will see next, Guava
provides an easier alternative.

Using the Suppliers class

As we have come to expect with Guava, there is a companion `Suppliers` class
with static methods for working with `Supplier` instances. In the previous example,
a new instance was returned with each invocation of the `get` method. If we wanted
to change our approach and return the same instance each time, `Suppliers` gives us
a few options.

Using the Suppliers.memoize method

The `Suppliers.memoize` method returns a `Supplier` instance that wraps a provided delegate `Supplier` instance. When the first call to `get` is executed, the call is passed to the delegate `Supplier` instance; it creates and returns the instance to the wrapping `Supplier` object. The wrapping `Supplier` object caches the instance before returning it to the caller. All subsequent calls to the `get` method return the cached instance. Here's how we
could use `Suppliers.memoize`:

```
Supplier<Predicate<String>> wrapped =
Suppliers.memoize(composedPredicateSupplier);
```

By adding just one line of code, we can now return the same instance of the `Predicate` object with each call to the `Supplier` object.

Using the Suppliers.memoizeWithExpiration method

The `Suppliers.memoizeWithExpiration` method works in the exact same manner as its `memoize` brother with the exception that after a given period of time when `get` is called, the wrapper `Supplier` object retrieves the instance from the delegate `Supplier`. object The wrapper `Supplier` instance then caches the instance for the given period of time. Take note that the instance is not held in a physical cache; rather the wrapping `Supplier` object keeps an instance variable that is set to the value returned by the delegate Supplier object. Here's an example:

```
Supplier<Predicate<String>> wrapped =
Suppliers.memoize(composedPredicateSupplier,10L,TimeUnit.MINUTES);
```

Here we've wrapped `Supplier` again and set the timeout to be 10 minutes. For `ComposedPredicateSupplier`, it won't make much difference; but for `Supplier` that is returning an object that could have changes, something retrieved from a database, for example, the `memoizeWithExpiration` method, could be very helpful.

> Using the `Supplier` interface with dependency injection is a powerful combination. However, if you are using Guice (a dependency injection framework from Google), it has a `Provider<T>` interface that provides the same functionality as the `Supplier<T>` interface. Of course, if you wanted to take advantage of the caching with expiration features, you would have to use the `Supplier` interface.

Summary

We've seen how Guava can add some functional aspects to Java with the `Function` and `Predicate` interfaces. The `Function` interface provides us with the ability to transform objects and the `Predicate` interface gives us a powerful mechanism for filtering. The `Functions` and `Predicates` classes also help us write code that is easier to maintain and much easier to change. `Suppliers` help by providing essential collaborating objects while completely hiding the details of how those objects are created. Combined with a dependency injection framework such as Spring or Guice, these interfaces will allow us to seamlessly change the behavior of our programs by simply providing a different implementation. In the next chapter, we dive into the workhorse of Google Guava: Collections.

4
Working with Collections

Collections are essential to any programming language. We simply cannot write a program of any significance without using collections. The Guava library has its history rooted in working with collections, starting out as google-collections. The Google Collections Library has long since been abandoned, and all the functionality from the original library has been merged into Guava. We can get a sense of the importance of working with collections just by looking at the number of classes in the `com.google.common.collect` package; by far, it contains the largest number of classes compared to the other packages in Guava. Given the size of the `com.google.common.collect` package, we simply won't be able to cover everything. But we will attempt to cover those things that are especially powerful and those that we are likely to need on a daily basis. Specifically, we will be covering the following things in this chapter:

- Classes with useful static methods for working with lists, maps, and sets
- The `Range` class used to represent the boundaries around a continuous set of values
- Immutable Collections
- Bimaps, which are maps where we can navigate from values to keys as well as the traditional key-to-value navigation
- The `Table` collection type, which is a very powerful collection that is a replacement for using a map of maps
- Multimaps, which allow us to have more than one value associated with a unique key
- The `FluentIterable` class, which presents a set of powerful interfaces for working with `Iterable` instances
- The `Ordering` class that gives us enhanced abilities when working with `Comparators`

The FluentIterable class

The `FluentIterable` class presents a powerful interface for working with `Iterable` instances in the **fluent** style of programming. The fluent programming style allows us to chain method calls together, making for a more readable code.

Using the FluentIterable.filter method

The `FluentIterable.filter` method takes a Predicateas an argument. Then every element is examined and retained if the given `Predicate` holds true for it. If no objects satisfy the Predicate, an empty `Iterable` will be returned. In this example, we are going to demonstrate using the `from` and `filter` methods:

```
@Before
public void setUp() {
    person1 = new Person("Wilma", "Flintstone", 30, "F");
    person2 = new Person("Fred", "Flintstone", 32, "M");
    person3 = new Person("Betty", "Rubble", 31, "F");
    person4 = new Person("Barney", "Rubble", 33, "M");
    personList = Lists.newArrayList(person1, person2, person3,
person4);
}


@Test
public void testFilter() throws Exception {
    Iterable<Person> personsFilteredByAge=
FluentIterable.from(personList).filter(new Predicate<Person>() {
        @Override
        public boolean apply(Person input) {
            return input.getAge() > 31;
        }
    });

    assertThat(Iterables.contains(filtered, person2),
is(true));
    assertThat(Iterables.contains(filtered, person4),
is(true));
    assertThat(Iterables.contains(filtered, person1),
is(false));
    assertThat(Iterables.contains(filtered, person3),
is(false));
}
```

In the `setUp` method, we create the `personList` list by calling the static factory's `Lists.newArrayList()` method with four `Person` objects. Then in `testFilter`, we create `personsFilteredByAge` by passing the `personList` parameter to the `FluentIterable.from()` method chained with the `filter` method with a `Predicate` parameter. In our `assertThat` statements, we see the use of the `Iterables.contains` method to verify the results. `Iterables` is a utility class for working with `Iterable` instances.

Using the FluentIterable.transform method

The `FluentIterable.transform` method is a mapping operation where `Function` is applied to each element. This yields a new iterable having the same size as the original one, composed of the transformed objects. This differs from the `filter` method, which may remove any or all of the original elements. Here we demonstrate the `transform` method, re-using the data created in the `setUp` method from the previous example:

```
@Test
    public void testTransform() throws Exception {
        List<String> transformedPersonList =
FluentIterable.from(personList).transform(new Function<Person,
String>() {
            @Override
            public String apply(Person input) {

                return Joiner.on('#').join(input.getLastName(),
input.getFirstName(), input.getAge());
            }
        }).toList();
        assertThat(transformed.get(1), is("Flintstone#Fred#32"));
    }
```

In this example, we are transforming each object in `personList` into a # delimited string composed of the last name, first name, and age of the given `Person` object. We have the `FluentIterable.from` method, this time chained with `transform` passing in `Function`, but we have also chained a third method, `toList`, which returns the final result as `List<String>`. There are also the `toSet`, `toMap`, `toSortedList`, and `toSortedSet` methods available. The `toMap` method considers the elements of the `FluentIterable` instance to be the keys, and requires `Function` to map values to those keys. Both the `toSortedList` and `toSortedSet` methods take a `Comparator` parameter to specify the order. There are several other methods not covered here, and given the very large number of classes that implement or extend the `Iterable` interface, `FluentIterable` is a very useful tool to have at our disposal.

Lists

Lists is a utility class for working with the List instances. One of the biggest conveniences provided is the ability to create new List instances:

```
List<Person> personList = Lists.newArrayList();
```

Using the Lists.partition method

The Lists.partition() method is an interesting method that returns sublists of size *n* from a given list. For example, assume that you have previously created four Person objects and have created List with the following static factory method in the Lists class:

```
List<Person> personList =
Lists.newArrayList(person1,person2,person3,person4);
```

Then we call the Lists.partition() method specifying two partitions:

```
List<List<Person>> subList = Lists.partition(personList,2);
```

In this example, the subList list would contain [[person1,person2],[person3, person4]]. The partition method returns consecutive sublists of the same size, with the exception of the last sublist, which may be smaller. For example, if 3 were passed in as the size for the sublist method, Lists.partition() would have returned [[person1,person2,person3],[person4]].

Sets

Sets is a utility class for working with Set instances. There are static factory methods for creating HashSets, LinkedHashSets (Set instances that guarantee items stay in the same order as they are added), and TreeSets (items are sorted by their natural order or by a provided Comparator). We are going to cover the methods in the Sets class that we can use for creating new permutations of a set (subsets and union), or operations that can inform us whether the Set instances have anything in common or not (difference and intersection). While there is a filter method, that functionality has already been covered and won't be repeated here.

Using the Sets.difference method

The `Sets.difference` method takes two set instance parameters and returns `SetView` of the elements found in the first set, but not in the second. `SetView` is a static, abstract inner class of the `Sets` class and represents an unmodifiable view of a given `Set` instance. Any elements that exist in the second set but not in the first set are not included. For example, the following would return a `SetView` instance with one element, `"1"`:

```
Set<String> s1 = Sets.newHashSet("1","2","3");
Set<String> s2 = Sets.newHashSet("2","3","4");
Sets.difference(s1,s2);
```

If we were to reverse the order of the arguments, a `SetVeiw` instance with one element, `"4"`, would have been returned.

Using the Sets.symmetricDifference method

The `Sets.symmetricDifference` method returns elements that are contained in one set or the other set, but not contained in both. The returned set is an unmodifiable view. Using the previous example, we have:

```
Set<String> s1 = Sets.newHashSet("1","2","3");
Set<String> s2 = Sets.newHashSet("2","3","4");
Sets.SetView setView = Sets.symmetricDifference(s1,s2);
//Would return [1,4]
```

Using the Sets.intersection method

The `Sets.intersection` method returns an unmodifiable `SetView` instance containing elements that are found in two `Set` instances. Let us take a look at the following example:

```
@Test
    public void testIntersection(){
        Set<String> s1 = Sets.newHashSet("1","2","3");
        Set<String> s2 = Sets.newHashSet("3","2","4");
        Sets.SetView<String> sv = Sets.intersection(s1,s2);
        assertThat(sv.size()==2 && sv.contains("2") &&
sv.contains("3"),is(true));
```

Using the Sets.union method

The `Sets.union` method takes two sets and returns a `SetView` instance that contains elements that are found in either set. Let us take a look at the following example:

```
@Test
    public void testUnion(){
        Set<String> s1 = Sets.newHashSet("1","2","3");
        Set<String> s2 = Sets.newHashSet("3","2","4");
        Sets.SetView<String> sv = Sets.union(s1,s2);
        assertThat(sv.size()==4 &&
                sv.contains("2") &&
                sv.contains("3") &&
                sv.contains("4") &&
                sv.contains("1"),is(true));
    }
```

Maps

Maps are one of the essential data structures we programmers use on a daily basis. Given their heavy usage, any method that makes creating and working with maps easier is bound to be a productivity booster to Java programmers. The `Maps` utility class in Guava offers such help. First we will examine methods that make it much easier to construct a map from an existing collection of objects. It's a very common practice to have a collection of objects and have the need to create a map of those objects, usually to serve as some sort of cache or to enable fast lookups. For the next example, let's assume we have a List of Book objects and we would like to store them in a map with the ISBN number as the key. First, a possible way of converting `List` into `Map` in Java is as follows:

```
List<Book> books = someService.getBooks();
Map<String,Book> bookMap = new HashMap<String,Book>()
for(Book book : books){
    bookMap.put(book.getIsbn(),book);
}
```

While the preceding code is straightforward, we can do better.

Using the Maps.uniqueIndex method

The `Maps.uniqueIndex` method takes either an iterable or iterator of a given type and `Function` as arguments. The elements represented by the iterator/iterable become the values for the map, while `Function` is applied to each element and generates the key for that element. So if we were to rework on our previous example, we would have something as follows:

```
List<Book> books = someService.getBooks();
Map<String,Book>bookMap = Maps.uniqueIndex(books.iterator(),new
Function<Book, String>(){
        @Override
        public String apply( Book input) {
                return input.getIsbn();
        }
    };)
```

In this example, we are providing the iterator from the books' `List` object and defining a function that extracts the ISBN number for each book, which will be used as the key for the `Book` object in the map. Although the example is using an anonymous class for `Function`, if we were to have `Function` passed in either by a method call or with dependency injection, we could easily change the algorithm for generating the key for the `Book` object, with no impact to the surrounding code.

Using the Maps.asMap method

While the `Maps.uniqueIndex` method uses `Function` to generate keys from the given values, the `Maps.asMap` method does the inverse operation. The `Maps.asMap` method takes a set of objects to be used as keys, and `Function` is applied to each key object to generate the value for entry into a map instance. There is another method, `Maps.toMap`, that takes the same arguments with the difference being `ImmutableMap` is returned instead of a view of the map. The significance of this is that the map returned from the `Maps.asMap` method would reflect any changes made to the original map, and the map returned from the `Maps.toMap` method would remain unchanged from changes to the original map.

Transforming maps

There are some great methods in the `Maps` class that are used to transform the map's values. The `Maps.transformEntries` method uses a `Maps.EntryTransformer` interface that derives a new value for the same key, based on the key and value from the original map. There is another method, `Maps.transformValues`, which uses `Function` that takes the map's original value and transforms it into a new value for the same key in the original map.

Multimaps

While maps are great data structures that are used constantly in programming, there are times when programmers need to associate more than one value with a given key. While we are free to create our own implementations of maps that have a list or set as a value, Guava makes it much easier. The static factory methods return map instances that give us the familiar semantics of the `put(key,value)` operation. The details of checking if a collection exists for the given key and creating one if necessary, then adding the value to that collection, are taken care of for us. Let's dive in and explore this powerful abstraction.

ArrayListMultimap

`ArrayListMulitmap` is a map that uses `ArrayList` to store the values for the given key. To create an `ArrayListMultimap` instance, we use one of the following methods:

- `ArrayListMultimap<String,String> multiMap = ArrayListMultimap.create();`

- `ArrayListMutilmap<String,String> multiMap = ArrayListMultimap.create(numExcpectedKeys,numExpectedValuesPer Key);`

- `ArrayListMulitmap<String,String> mulitMap = ArrayListMultimap.create(listMultiMap);`

The first option simply creates an empty `ArrayListMultimap` instance with the default sizes for the keys and `ArrayList` value. The second method sets the initial size for the expected number of keys and the expected size of `ArrayList` for holding the values. The last method simply creates a new `ArrayListMultimap` instance using the keys and values of the supplied `Multimap` parameter. Let's demonstrate how to use `ArrayListMultimap` with the following example:

```
@Test
    public void testArrayListMultiMap(){
```

```
        ArrayListMultimap<String,String> multiMap =
ArrayListMultimap.create();
        multiMap.put("Foo","1");
        multiMap.put("Foo","2");
        multiMap.put("Foo","3");
        List<String> expected = Lists.newArrayList("1","2","3");
        assertEquals(multiMap.get("Foo"),expected);
}
```

Here we are creating a new multimap and then adding three values for the same key. Note that we just create the multimap and then start adding keys and values with the familiar put method call. Finally we call get for the Foo key and confirm that it returned a List with the expected values.

Now let's consider another usage. What do we think would happen if we try to add the same key-value pair more than once? Consider the following example as a unit test and think about whether it's going to pass or not:

```
@Test
    public void testArrayListMultimapSameKeyValue(){
        ArrayListMultimap<String,String> multiMap =
ArrayListMultimap.create();
        multiMap.put("Bar","1");
        multiMap.put("Bar","2");
        multiMap.put("Bar","3");
        multiMap.put("Bar","3");
        multiMap.put("Bar","3");
        List<String> expected = Lists.
newArrayList("1","2","3","3","3");
        assertEquals(multiMap.get("Bar"),expected);
    }
```

Considering that a List does not force its elements to be unique, the unit test shown previously passes. We are simply adding another element to a List that is associated with a given key. Now it's time for a short quiz. Consider the following multimap:

```
        multiMap.put("Foo","1");
        multiMap.put("Foo","2");
        multiMap.put("Foo","3");
        multiMap.put("Bar","1");
        multiMap.put("Bar","2");
        multiMap.put("Bar","3");
```

What is the result of the `multiMap.size()` call? It's 6, not 2. The call to `size()` takes into account all values found in each List, and not the total number of `List` instances in the map. Additionally, a call to `values()` returns a collection containing all six values, not a collection containing two lists with three elements each. While this may seem puzzling at first, we need to remember that the multimap is not a true map. But if we need typical map behavior, we would do the following:

```
Map<String,Collection<String>> map = multiMap.asMap();
```

The call to `asMap()` returns a map where each key points to the corresponding collection in the original multimap. The returned map is a live view, and changes to the view would be reflected in the underlying multimap. Also, keep in mind that the returned map would not support the `put(key,value)` call as before. We've spent a fair amount of time talking about `ArrayListMultimap`, but there are other implementations of the multimap.

HashMultimap

`HashMultimap` is based on hash tables. Unlike `ArrayListMultimap`, inserting the same key-value pair multiple times is not supported. Let us take a look at the following example:

```
        HashMultimap<String,String> multiMap =
    HashMultimap.create();
        multiMap.put("Bar","1");
        multiMap.put("Bar","2");
        multiMap.put("Bar","3");
        multiMap.put("Bar","3");
        multiMap.put("Bar","3");
```

In this example, we are inserting the same value for the `Bar` key three times. However, when we call `multiMap.size()`, 3 is returned, as only distinct key-value pairs are kept. Apart from not supporting duplicate key-value inserts, the functionality is close enough that we don't need to repeat it.

Before we move on, it's worth mentioning some of the other implementations of multimap. First, there are three immutable implementations: `ImmutableListMultimap`, `ImmutableMultimap`, and `ImmutableSetMultimap`. There is `LinkedHashMultimap`, which returns collections for a given key that have the values in the same order as they were inserted. Finally, we have `TreeMultimap` that keeps the keys and values sorted by their natural order or the order specified by a comparator.

BiMap

Next to being able to have multiple values for a key in a map, is the ability to navigate from a value to a key in a map. The bimap gives us that functionality. The bimap is unique, in that it keeps the values unique in the map as well as the keys, which is a prerequisite to *invert* the map and navigate from a value to a key. The bimap operates differently when it comes to adding values into the map. Let us take a look at the following example:

```
BiMap<String,String> biMap = HashBiMap.create();
biMap.put("1","Tom");
//This call causes an IllegalArgumentException to be
thrown!
biMap.put("2","Tom");
```

In this example, we are adding two different keys with the same value, which is an expected behavior for a traditional map. But when using a bimap, inserting a new key with a value that already exists in the map causes `IllegalArgumentException` to be thrown.

Using the BiMap.forcePut method

In order to add the same value with a different key, we need to call `forcePut(key,value)`. The `BiMap.forcePut` call will quietly remove the map entry with the same value before placing the key-value pair in the map. Obviously, if it's the same key and value, the net effect on the map is nothing. However, if the value is the same and the key is different, the previous key is discarded. The following is a simple unit test to illustrate the point:

```
@Test
public void testBiMapForcePut() throws Exception {
    BiMap<String,String> biMap = HashBiMap.create();
    biMap.put("1","Tom");
    biMap.forcePut("2","Tom");
    assertThat(biMap.containsKey("1"),is(false));
    assertThat(biMap.containsKey("2"),is(true));
}
```

What we are doing in the previous test is adding the value Tom with the key 1. We then add the Tom value again with a key of 2, this time using the forcePut method. In the preceding example, the original key (1) is discarded and we now have a new key (2) pointing to the value of Tom. This behavior makes complete sense. Since the values map to keys when the inverse method is called, one of the values (a previous key) would be overwritten. So using the forcePut method is an explicit way of stating that we would like to replace the current key as opposed to getting unexpected behavior.

Using the BiMap.inverse method

Now let's take a look at using the inverse method:

```
@Test
public void testBiMapInverse() throws Exception {
    BiMap<String,String> biMap = HashBiMap.create();
    biMap.put("1","Tom");
    biMap.put("2","Harry");
    assertThat(biMap.get("1"),is("Tom"));
    assertThat(biMap.get("2"),is("Harry"));
    BiMap<String,String> inverseMap = biMap.inverse();
    assertThat(inverseMap.get("Tom"),is("1"));
    assertThat(inverseMap.get("Harry"),is("2"));
}
```

In the preceding example, we are adding key-value pairs of ("1","Tom") and ("2","Harry") and asserting that "1" points to the value "Tom" and "2" points to the value 'Harry". Then we call inverse on the original BiMap and assert that "Tom" points to "1" and "Harry" points to "2". Although we only covered the HashBiMap method here, there are also implementations of EnumBiMap, EnumHashBiMap, and ImmutableBiMap.

Table

Maps are very powerful collections that are commonly used in programming. But there are times when a single map is not enough; we need to have a map of maps. While very useful, creating and using them in Java can be cumbersome. Fortunately, Guava has provided a table collection. A table is a collection that takes two keys, a row, and a column, and maps those keys to a single value. While not explicitly called out as a map of maps, however, the table gives us the desired functionality and is much easier to use.

There are several implementations of a table, and for our examples, we will be working with `HashBasedTable`, which stores data in `Map<R, Map<C, V>>`. Creating an instance of `HashBasedTable` comes with the ease we have come to expect from working with Guava:

```
HashBasedTable<Integer,Integer,String> table =
HashBasedTable.create();
//Creating table with 5 rows and columns initially
HashBasedTable<Integer,Integer,String> table =
HashBasedTable.create(5,5);

//Creating a table from an existing table
HashBasedTable<Integer,Integer,String> table =
HashBasedTable.create(anotherTable);
```

Table operations

The following are some examples of common operations we do with a `Table` instance:

```
HashBasedTable<Integer,Integer,String> table =
HashBasedTable.create();

table.put(1,1,"Rook");
table.put(1,2,"Knight");
table.put(1,3,"Bishop");


boolean contains11 = table.contains(1,1);
boolean containColumn2 = table.containsColumn(2);
boolean containsRow1 = table.containsRow(1);
boolan containsRook = table.containsValue("Rook");
table.remove(1,3);
table.get(3,4);
```

The previous example methods are exactly what we would expect to see in a map, but consider the concise manner we can go about accessing values as opposed to doing so with a traditional map of maps structure.

Table views

The table provides some great methods for obtaining different views of the underlying data in the table:

```
Map<Integer,String> columnMap = table.column(1);
Map<Integer,String> rowMap = table.row(2);
```

The `column` method returns a map where the keys are all row-value mappings with the given column's key value. The `row` method returns the converse, returning column-value mappings with the given row's key value. The maps returned are live views and change to `columnMap` and `rowMap`, or the original table would be reflected in the other. There are other implementations of the table we should discuss briefly as follows:

1. `ArrayTable` is an implementation of the table backed by a two-dimensional array.

2. There is an `ImmutableTable` implementation. Since `ImmutableTable` can't be updated after it's created, the row, key, and values are added using `ImmutableTable.Builder`, which leverages a fluent interface for ease of construction.

3. A `TreeBasedTable` table where the row and column keys are ordered, either by the natural order or by specified comparators for the row and column keys.

This concludes our discussion of the many map implementations found in Guava, and we now move on to other classes found in the `com.google.common.collect` package.

Range

The `Range` class allows us to create a specific interval or span of values with defined endpoints, and works with `Comparable` types. The `Range` objects can define endpoints that are either inclusive (closed), which includes the end value of the `Range` instance, or exclusive (open), which does not include the end value of the `Range` instance. `Range` is better understood with a code example as follows:

```
Range<Integer> numberRange = Range.closed(1,10);
//both return true meaning inclusive
numberRange.contains(10);
numberRange.contains(1);
```

```
Range<Integer> numberRange = Range.open(1,10);
//both return false meaning exclusive
numberRange.contains(10);
numberRange.contains(1);
```

We can create `Range` objects with a variety of boundary conditions such as
`openClosed`, `closedOpen`, `greaterThan`, `atLeast`, `lessThan`, and `atMost`.
All of the listed conditions mentioned in this list are static factory methods
that return the desired range.

Ranges with arbitrary comparable objects

Since `Range` objects work with any object that implements the `Comparable`
interface, it makes it easy to create a filter for working with only those objects
that fall within our desired boundaries. For example, consider the `Person` class
we introduced before:

```
public class Person implements Comparable<Person> {

    private String firstName;
    private String lastName;
    private int age;
    private String sex;


    @Override
    public int compareTo(Person o) {
        return ComparisonChain.start().
                compare(this.firstName,o.getFirstName()).
                compare(this.lastName,o.getLastName()).
                compare(this.age,o.getAge()).
                compare(this.sex,o.getSex()).result();
    }
}
```

We would like to create a `Range` instance for the `Person` objects where the age is
between 35 and 50. But if you look at the `compareTo` method, we have a slight
problem; it includes all the fields in the object. To solve this problem, we are going
to leverage the fact that the `Range` object implements the `Predicate` interface.
Additionally, we are going to use the `Predicates.compose` method to create a new
`Predicate` composed of `Range` and `Function`. First, let's define our `Range` instance:

```
Range<Integer> ageRange = Range.closed(35,50);
```

Next, we will create `Function` that accepts a `Person` object and returns the age:

```
Function<Person,Integer> ageFunction = new Function<Person,
Integer>() {
        @Override
        public Integer apply(Person person) {
            return person.getAge();
        }
    };
```

Finally, we create our composed `Predicate`:

```
Predicate<Person> predicate =
Predicates.compose(ageRange,ageFunction);
```

Now we could have just as easily created a `Predicate` instance to validate an age range. But by using composition, we can substitute either a new `Range` object or a new `Comparable` object. The `Range` object presents an opportunity to perform powerful operations and make other tasks, for example, filtering, more concise.

Immutable collections

Throughout this chapter, we have seen several examples of creating collections. But most, if not all, of the methods we have looked at so far return mutable collections. However, if we don't explicitly have a need for a mutable collection, we should always favor using an immutable one. First of all, immutable collections are completely thread-safe. Secondly, they offer protection from unknown users who may try to access your code. Fortunately, Guava provides a vast selection of immutable collections. As a matter of fact, for each collection type we have covered in this chapter, there is a suitable immutable version.

Creating immutable collection instances

Since the functionality is really no different from the collection's mutable counterparts, we will only cover the one major difference between the two, by using the `Builder` pattern to create an instance. All of the Guava immutable collections have a static nested `Builder` class that uses the fluent interface approach to create the desired instance. Let's use `ImmutableListMultimap.Builder` in the following example:

```
MultiMap<Integer,String> map = new
ImmutableListMultimap.Builder<Integer,String>()
.put(1,"Foo")
.putAll(2,"Foo","Bar","Baz")
```

```
.putAll(4,"Huey","Duey","Luey")
.put(3,"Single").build();
```

In this example, we are simply instantiating new `Builder`, adding the required keys and values, and then calling the `build` method at the end, which returns `ImmutableListMultiMap`.

Ordering

Sorting collections is a key issue in programming. Given the fact that useful collection abstractions are essential to programming, it also stands to reason that good sorting tools are just as essential. The `Ordering` class provides us with tools that we need for applying different sorting techniques powerfully and concisely. `Ordering` is an abstract class. While it implements the `Comparator` interface, `Ordering` has the `compare` method declared as `abstract`.

Creating an Ordering instance

There are two ways in which you can create an instance of `Ordering`:

- Creating a new instance and providing an implementation for the `compare` method.
- Using the static `Ordering.from` method that creates an instance of `Ordering` from an existing `Comparator`.

How we go about it depends on whether we need to explicitly create a new `Comparator` instance, or have an existing one where we want to take advantage of the extra features the `Ordering` class provides.

Reverse sorting

Consider we have the following `Comparator` instance for the `City` objects to sort by the population size:

```
public class CityByPopluation implements Comparator<City> {

    @Override
    public int compare(City city1, City city2) {
        return Ints.compare(city1.getPopulation(),city2.
getPopulation());
    }
}
```

If we were to use the CityByPopulation comparator to sort a collection of City objects, the list would be sorted in its natural order, from smallest to largest. But what if we wanted to have the list sorted from largest to smallest? This can be done easily:

```
Ordering.from(cityByPopluation).reverse();
```

What we are doing in this example is creating a new Ordering object from the existing CityByPopulation comparator and specifying that the sort order is to be reversed, from largest to smallest.

Accounting for null

When sorting, we always need to consider how we will treat null values. Do we put them first or last? Ordering makes either decision very easy to implement:

```
Ordering.from(comparator).nullsFirst();
```

In the preceding example, we are creating an instance of Ordering and immediately calling the nullsFirst method, which returns an Ordering instance that treats the null values as less than any other value in the collection, and as a result, places them first in the list. There is also a corresponding Ordering.nullsLast call, which places nulls last in the collection when sorted.

Secondary sorting

Often when sorting objects, we need to handle the case of our sorting criterion being equal, and we define a secondary sorting criterion. Previously, we defined Comparator for sorting the City objects by population, now we have another Comparator:

```
public class CityByRainfall implements Comparator<City> {

    @Override
    public int compare(City city1, City city2) {
            return Doubles.compare(city1.getAverageRainfall(),city2.
getAverageRainfal
l());
    }
}
```

In the preceding code, `Comparator` will sort the `City` objects by their average rainfall per year. Here's how we can use an additional `Comparator`:

```
Ordering.from(cityByPopulation).compound(cityByRainfall);
```

Here we are creating an `Ordering` instance from `CityByPopulationComparator`. We are then calling the `compound` method, which takes another `CityByRainfall` comparator in this case. Now when the `City` objects that have the same population are being sorted, the `Ordering` instance will delegate to the secondary comparator. Here's an example:

```
@Test
    public void testSecondarySort(){
        City city1 = cityBuilder.population(100000).
averageRainfall(55.0).build();
        City city2 = cityBuilder.population(100000).
averageRainfall(45.0).build();
        City city3 = cityBuilder.population(100000).
averageRainfall(33.8).build();
        List<City> cities = Lists.newArrayList(city1,city2,city3);
        Ordering<City> secondaryOrdering = Ordering.
from(cityByPopulation).compound(cityByRainfall);
        Collections.sort(cities,secondaryOrdering);
        assertThat(cities.get(0),is(city3));
    }
```

Retrieving minimum and maximum values

Finally, we look at how `Ordering` allows us to easily retrieve the minimum or maximum values from a collection.

```
Ordering<City> ordering = Ordering.from(cityByPopluation);
List<City> topFive = ordering.greatestOf(cityList,5);
List<City> bottomThree = ordering.leastOf(cityList,3);
```

Here we are creating an `Ordering` instance from the now familiar `CityByPopulation` comparator. We then call the `greatestOf` method with a list of `City` objects and an integer. The `Ordering.greatestOf` method will return the *n* greatest elements (five greatest elements in this case). The second example, `leastOf`, takes the same arguments, but performs the opposite action, returning the *n* least elements (three in our preceding example). While we are using lists in the previous examples, the `greatestOf` and `leastOf` methods also accept `Iterable<T>`. While we won't show examples here, `Ordering` also has methods that will retrieve a maximum or minimum value.

Summary

We've learned about the very useful and versatile FluentIterable class. We saw how we can have more than one value associated with a given key with the multimap, and how we can use the bimap to navigate from values to keys. We covered the Table collection, which is a great abstraction for a map of maps. We learned about the Range object and how we can use it to determine the boundaries of the values contained in a collection. Immutable collections are a very important part of our programming arsenal, and we learned the importance of using them as well as creating an immutable collection. Finally we learned about the powerful Ordering class, which makes the important task of sorting easier. Next, we take a look at the tools that Guava provides us for working with concurrency.

5
Concurrency

As Guava has grown from methods to help you work from Java collections to an all-purpose library, one of the areas where Guava really shines is concurrency. When Java 5 introduced the `java.util.concurrent` package, concurrency in Java became easier to implement. Guava builds on top of those constructs. The classes found in `com.google.util.concurrent` give us some very useful features in addition to those already found in Java's `java.util.concurrent` package.

In this chapter we are going to cover:

- The `Monitor` class that functions as a Mutex, ensuring serial access to the defined areas in our code, much like the synchronized keyword but with much easier semantics and some useful additional features.

- The `ListenableFuture` class that functions the same way the `Listenable` class does from Java, with the exception that we can register a callback method to run once the `Future` has itself been completed.

- The `FutureCallback` class that gives us access to the result of a `Future` task allowing us to handle success and failure scenarios.

- The `SettableFuture`, `AsyncFunction`, and `FutureFallback` classes that are useful utility classes we can use when working with `Future` instances and doing asynchronous transformation of objects.

- The `Futures` class that is a class with useful static methods for working with `Future` instances.

- The `RateLimiter` class that restricts how often threads can access a resource. It is very much like a semaphore but instead of limiting access by a total number of threads, the `RateLimiter` class restricts access based on time.

[
There are several classes we are going to cover in this chapter that have an `@Beta` annotation indicating that the functionality of that class may be subject to change in a future release.
]

Synchronizing threads

Since Java offers the ability to have multiple threads running in a program, there are occasions when we need to restrict the access (synchronize) so that only one thread can access parts of our code at any given time. Java provides the synchronized keyword that accomplishes this goal of serial access. But using `synchronized` has some issues. First, if we need to call `wait()` on a thread, we must remember to use a `while` loop:

```
while(someCondition){
  try {
     wait();
  } catch (InterruptedException e) {
    //In this case we don't care, but we may want
    //to propagate with Thread.interrupt()
   }
}
```

Second, if we have more than one condition that can cause a thread to go into a wait state, we must call `notifyAll()`, as we don't have the ability to notify threads for specific conditions. Using `notifyAll()` instead of `notify()` is less desirable due to the thrashing effect it has of waking up all the threads to compete for a lock when only one will do so. Java 5 introduced the `ReentrantLock` class and the ability to create a condition. We can achieve finer granularity by using the `ReentrantLock.newCondition()` method and now can wake up a single thread waiting on a particular condition to occur with a `Condition.signal()` call (analogous to `notify()`), although there is a `Condition.signalAll()` method that has the same thrashing effect as calling `notifyAll()`. But we still have the somewhat counterintuitive `while` loop to contend with:

```
while(list.isEmpty()){
    Condition.await();
}
```

Fortunately, Guava has an answer to this issue, the `Monitor` class.

Monitor

The `Monitor` class from Guava gives us a solution that allows multiple conditions and completely eliminates the possibility of notifying all threads by switching from an explicit notification system to an implicit one. Let's take a look at an example:

```
public class MonitorSample {
    private List<String> list = new ArrayList<String>();
    private static final int MAX_SIZE = 10;

    private Monitor monitor = new Monitor();
    private Monitor.Guard listBelowCapacity = new
Monitor.Guard(monitor) {
        @Override
        public boolean isSatisfied() {
            return list.size() < MAX_SIZE;
        }
    };

    public void addToList(String item) throws InterruptedException
{
        monitor.enterWhen(listBelowCapacity);
        try {
            list.add(item);
        } finally {
            monitor.leave();
        }
    }
}
```

Let's go over the interesting parts of our example. First we are creating a new instance of a `Monitor` class. Next we use our newly created `Monitor` instance to construct an instance of a `Guard` class, which has one abstract method called `isSatisfied` that returns a boolean. Here our `Guard` instance returns true when our `List` instance contains fewer than ten items. Finally in the `addToList` method, a thread will enter the `Monitor` and add an item to the list when our `Guard` condition evaluates to true, otherwise, the thread will wait. Notice the more readable `enterWhen` method that will allow a thread to enter the block when the `Guard` condition is satisfied. Also take note that we are not explicitly signaling any threads; it's entirely implied by the `Guard` condition being satisfied. We've explained the code example but now let's dig into the `Monitor` class a little more.

Monitor explained

When a thread enters a `Monitor` block, it is considered to occupy that `Monitor` instance, and once the thread leaves, it no longer occupies the `Monitor` block. Only one thread can enter a `Monitor` block at any time. The semantics are the same as using `synchronized` or `ReentrantLocks`; a thread enters and no other thread can enter that area until the current thread releases the lock or in our case, leaves the `Monitor` block. The same thread can enter and exit the same `Monitor` block any number of times but each entry must be followed by an exit.

Monitor best practice

`Monitor` methods that return boolean values should always be used within an `if` statement that contains a `try`/`finally` block to ensure the thread will always be able to exit the `Monitor` block.

```
if (monitor.enterIf(guardCondition)) {
    try {
        doWork();
} finally {
    monitor.leave();
    }
}
```

For `Monitor` methods that don't return any values, the method class should immediately be followed by a `try`/`finally` block as follows:

```
monitor.enterWhen(guardCondition);
try {
    doWork();
} finally {
    monitor.leave()
}
```

Different Monitor access methods

While the `Monitor` class has several methods for entering a monitor, there are five basic types that we will describe here.

1. `Monitor.enter`: The `Monitor.enter` method will attempt to enter a monitor and will block indefinitely until the thread enters the monitor.

2. `Monitor.enterIf`: The `Monitor.enterIf` method takes `Monitor.Guard` as an argument and will block to enter the monitor. Once it enters the monitor, it will not wait for the condition to be satisfied, but it will return a boolean indicating whether the `Monitor` block was entered.

3. `Monitor.enterWhen`: The `Monitor.enterWhen` method also takes `Monitor.Guard` as an argument and blocks, waiting to enter the monitor. However, once the lock is obtained, it will wait indefinitely for the condition to be satisfied.

4. `Monitor.tryEnter`: The `Monitor.tryEnter` method will attempt to access the monitor but if it is already occupied by another thread, it will not wait at all to obtain the lock but will return a boolean indicating whether the `Monitor` block was entered.

5. `Monitor.tryEnterIf`: The `Monitor.tryEnterIf` method attempts to immediately enter the monitor only if the lock is available and the condition is satisfied; otherwise, it will not wait for the lock or the condition to be satisfied but will return a boolean indicating whether the `Monitor` block was entered.

All of the methods we just saw also have variations that take arguments (`long` and `TimeUnit`) to specify an amount of time needed to wait to acquire the lock, the condition to be satisfied, or both. While there are several ways to enter a `Monitor` block, it's probably a good idea to use one of the timed versions and handle the condition when the lock is unavailable, or the condition never seems to be satisfied.

ListenableFuture

Java 5 introduced several important concurrent constructs. One of those is the `Future` object. A `Future` object represents the result of an asynchronous operation. Here's an example:

```
ExecutorService executor = Executors.newCachedThreadPool();
Future<Integer> future = executor.submit(new Callable<Integer>(){
                    public Integer call() throws Exception{
                        return service.getCount();
                    }
                });
//Retrieve the value of computation
Integer count = future.get();
```

In our example here, we are submitting a `Callable` object to the `ExecutorService` instance. The `ExecutorService` instance immediately returns the `Future` object; however, that does not imply the task is done. To retrieve the result, we call `future.get()`, which may block if the task is not completed. The `ListenableFuture` interface extends the `Future` interface by allowing us to register a callback to be executed automatically once the submitted task is completed. We accomplish this by calling the `ListenableFuture.addListener` method that takes a `Runnable` instance and an `ExecutorService` object, which could be the same `Executor` instance the original task was submitted to or another `ExecutorService` instance entirely.

Obtaining a ListenableFuture interface

As we have seen, the ExecutorService interface returns a Future object when a Callable object is submitted. How do we go about getting a ListenableFuture instance so we can set our callback method? We will wrap our ExecutorService object with a ListentingExecutorService interface by doing the following:

```
ListneningExecutorService service =
MoreExecutors.listeningDecorator(executorService);
```

Here we are using the MoreExecutors class that contains static methods for working with Executor, ExecutorService and ThreadPool instances. Here's an example that puts all of this together:

```
executorService =
MoreExecutors.listeningDecorator(Executors.newFixedThreadPool(NUM_
THREADS));

ListenableFuture<String> listenableFuture =
executorService.submit(new Callable<String>()…);

    listenableFuture.addListener(new Runnable() {
            @Override
            public void run() {
                methodToRunOnFutureTaskCompletion();

            }
        }, executorService);
```

Let's walk through the steps here. First we are taking an ExecutorService instance created from a fixed size thread pool and wrapping it with a ListeningExecutorService instance. Then we are submitting our Callable object to ListeningExecutorService and getting back our ListenableFuture instance. Finally we add a listener to run once the original task is completed. It's worth noting at this point that if the task is completed by the time we set the callback method, it will be executed immediately. There is a small limitation to the ListenableFuture. addListener method approach; we have no access to the returned object, and we can't specify different methods to run for success or failure conditions. Fortunately, we have an option that gives us that ability.

FutureCallback

The FutureCallback interface specifies the onSuccess and onFailure methods. The onSuccess method takes the result of the Future instance as an argument so we have access to the result of our task.

Using the FutureCallback

Using the FutureCallback interface is straightforward and works in a similar manner to registering a callback on the ListenableFuture interface, except we don't add FutureCallback directly to ListenbleFuture. Instead, we use the Futures.addCallback method. The Futures class is a collection of static-utility methods for working with Future instances and will be covered later in this chapter. Let's look at an example. First consider a very simple implementation of the FutureCallback interface:

```java
public class FutureCallbackImpl implements FutureCallback<String> {

    private StringBuilder builder = new StringBuilder();

    @Override
    public void onSuccess(String result) {
        builder.append(result).append(" successfully");

    }

    @Override
    public void onFailure(Throwable t) {
        builder.append(t.toString());
    }

    public String getCallbackResult() {
        return builder.toString();
    }
}
```

Here we are capturing the result in `onSuccess` and appending the text `"successfully"` to whatever the result was. In the event of a failure, we are getting the error message from the `Throwable` object. Now here's an example of putting all the pieces together:

```
ListenableFuture<String> futureTask = executorService.submit
(new Callable<String>(){
 @Override
  public String call() throws Exception{
        return "Task completed";
      }
    });

FutureCallbackImpl callback = new FutureCallbackImpl();
Futures.addCallback(futureTask, callback);
callback.getCallbackResult();
//Assuming success, would return "Task completed successfully"
```

In this example, we've created our `ListenableFuture` interface and an instance of a `FutureCallback` interface and registered it to be executed once our `ListenableFuture` instance is completed. The fact that we are accessing the result directly is strictly for an example. Typically, we would not want to access the result from the `FutureCallback` instance but would rather let `FutureCallback` handle the result asynchronously on its own. If the `FutureCallback` instance you are providing is going to perform any expensive operations, it's a good idea to use the following signature for the `Futures.addCallback` method:

```
Futures.addCallback(futureTask,callback,executorService);
```

By using this signature, the `FutureCallback` operation will be executed on a thread from the supplied `ExecutorService` parameter. Otherwise, the thread that executed the initial `ListenableFuture` instance would execute the `FutureCallback` operation behaving much like the `ThreadPoolExecutor.CallerRunsPolicy` executor service, which states that the task will be run on the caller's thread.

SettableFuture

The `SettableFuture` class is a `ListenableFuture` interface that we can use to set the value to be returned, or we can set `ListenableFuture` to `Fail` with a given exception. A `SettableFuture` instance is created by calling the static `create` method. Here's an example:

```
SettableFuture<String> sf = SettableFuture.create();

//Set a value to return
```

```
sf.set("Success");

//Or set a failure Exception
sf.setException(someException);
```

Here we are creating an instance of a SettableFuture class. Then if we wanted to set a value to be returned, we would call the set method and pass in an instance of the type expected to be returned by the Future instance. Or, if we wanted to set an exception that caused an error for this Future instance, we would pass in an instance of the appropriate exception. The SettableFuture class is very valuable for cases when you have a method that returns a Future instance, but you already have the value to be returned and you don't need to run an asynchronous task. We will see in the next section just how we can use the SettableFuture class.

AsyncFunction

The AsyncFunction interface is closely related to the Function interface we covered in *Chapter 3, Functional Programming with Guava*. Both accept an input object. The difference is that the AsyncFunction interface returns ListenableFuture as an output object. We call the ListenableFuture.get method when we retrieve the transformation result of the AsyncFunction interface. The AsyncFunction interface is used when we want to perform our transformation asynchronously without having a blocking call (although calling the Future.get method could block if the task has not been completed). But the AsyncFunction interface is not required to perform its transformation asynchronously; it's only required to return a Future instance. Let's look at an example in the following code:

```
public class AsyncFuntionSample implements
AsyncFunction<Long,String> {

    private ConcurrentMap<Long,String> map = Maps.newConcurrentMap();
    private ListeningExecutorService listeningExecutorService;




    @Override
    public ListenableFuture<String> apply(final Long input) throws
Exception {
        if(map.containsKey(input)) {
            SettableFuture<String> listenableFuture = SettableFuture.
create();
            listenableFuture.set(map.get(input));
            return listenableFuture;
```

```
        }else{
             return listeningExecutorService.submit(new
    Callable<String>(){
                   @Override
                   public String call() throws Exception {
                        String retrieved = service.get(input);
                        map.putIfAbsent (input,retrieved);
                        return retrieved;
                   }
             });
        }


    }
```

Here is our class that implements the AsyncFunction interface and contains an instance of ConcurrentHashMap. When we call the apply method, we would first look in our map for the value, given that the input object is considered as a key. If we find the value in the map, we use the SettableFuture class to create a Future object and set the value with the retrieved value from the map. Otherwise, we return the Future object that resulted from submitting Callable to ExecutorService (also putting the retrieved value in the map for the given key).

FutureFallback

The FutureFallback interface is used as a backup or a default value for a Future instance that has failed. FutureFallback is an interface with one method, create(Throwable t).

By accepting a Throwable instance, we can decide whether we should attempt to recover, return a default value, or propagate the exception. Consider the following example:

```
    public class FutureFallbackImpl implements FutureFallback<String>
    {

        @Override
        public ListenableFuture<String> create(Throwable t) throws
    Exception {
             if (t instanceof FileNotFoundException) {
                  SettableFuture<String> settableFuture =
    SettableFuture.create();
                  settableFuture.set("Not Found");
```

```
        return settableFuture;
    }
    throw new Exception(t);
    }
}
```

In this simple example, assume we were trying to asynchronously retrieve the name of a file, but if it's not found, we don't care (for the sake of the example); so, we create a `Future` object and set the value to `Not Found`. Otherwise, we just propagate the exception.

Futures

`Futures` is a utility class for working with `Future` instances. While there are many methods available, we are going to concentrate on the methods that utilize topics we've covered in this chapter: `AsyncFunctions` and `FutureFallbacks`. We've already seen some of the methods provided by the `Futures` class, such as the `Futures.addCallback` method used to attach a `FutureCallback` instance to run after a `ListenableFuture` instance has completed its task.

Asynchronous Transforms

We learned about the `AsyncFunction` interface in this chapter and how it can be used to asynchronously transform an input object. The `Futures` class has a `transform` method that makes it easy for us to use an `AsyncFunction` interface:

```
ListenableFuture<Person> lf =
Futures.transform(ListenableFuture<String> f,
AsyncFunction<String,Person> af);
```

Here the `Futures.transform` method returns a `ListenableFuture` instance whose result is obtained by performing an asynchronous transformation on the result from `ListenableFuture` passed into the function.

Applying FutureFallbacks

We also learned about `FutureFallback` interfaces and how they can provide us with the ability to handle errors from `ListenableFuture`. The `Futures.withFallback` method is a seamless way to apply `FutureFallback`, and is shown as follows:

```
ListenableFuture<String> lf =
Futures.withFallback(ListenableFuture<String> f,
FutureFallback<String> fb);
```

In this example, the returned `ListenableFuture` instance will have the result of the given `ListenableFuture`, if successful, or the result of the `FutureFallback` implementation.

In both the previous examples, we also have the option of using an overloaded method that takes `ExceutorService` to perform the action of `AsyncFunction` or `FutureFallback`.

There are several other methods for working with `Future` instances in the `Futures` class but going over more of them is left as an exercise for the reader.

RateLimiter

The `RateLimiter` class operates somewhat like a semaphore but instead of restricting access by the number of concurrent threads, the `RateLimiter` class restricts access by time, meaning how many threads can access a resource per second. We create a `RateLimiter` instance by doing the following:

```
RateLimiter limiter = RateLimiter.create(4.0);
```

Here we are calling the `create` method and passing in a double, `4.0`, specifying we don't want more than four tasks submitted per second. We use the `RateLimiter` class that is placed right before the call where we want to restrict the rate at which it is called. It is used in the same way we would use a semaphore. It is shown as follows:

```
limiter.acquire();
executor.submit(runnable);
```

In this example, we are calling the `acquire` method, which blocks until it can get a **permit** and access the resource. If we don't want to block at all, we could do the following:

```
If(limiter.tryAcquire()){
    doSomething();
}else{
    //Boo can't get in
    doSomethingElse();
}
```

Here we are calling `tryAcquire`, which gets a **permit** if one is available, otherwise, we immediately execute the next line of code. The `tryAcquire` method returns true if the permit was obtained, and false if otherwise. There is also a version of `tryAcquire`, where we can specify a time-out where the call will block for the given amount of time.

Summary

In this chapter, we've covered how to use the `Monitor` class to simplify our synchronization needs. We explored the `ListenableFuture` interface that allows us to specify a callback to run once the asynchronous task is completed. We learned how to use the `FutureCallback` class, and the `AsyncFunction` interface to asynchronously transform a value, and how the `FutureFallback` class allows us to handle errors from a `Future` interface that has failed. The `Futures` class provides us with great utility methods for working with instances of the `Future` interface. Finally we learned about the `RateLimiter` class. In the next chapter, we will cover the great caching tools offered by Guava.

6
Guava Cache

In software development, caching is a very important topic. If we are working on anything other than the simplest of programs, it's next to impossible to not find yourself in need of some sort of caching mechanism. Even if you need a map to look up static values, it's still a cache; but most of us don't see it that way. Caching in Guava gives us more power and flexibility than using plain `HashMap` but is not as robust as EHCache or Memcached. In this chapter, we are going to cover the caching functionality provided by Guava. We are going to elaborate more on the following topics:

- The `MapMaker` class for creating `ConcurrentMap` instances
- The `CacheBuilder` class that creates `LoadingCache` and `Cache` instances with a fluent builder API
- The `CacheBuilderSpec` class that creates a `CacheBuilder` instance from a formatted string
- The `CacheLoader` class that is used by a `LoadingCache` instance to retrieve a single value for a given key
- The `CacheStats` class that provides statistics of the performance of the cache
- The `RemovalListener` class that receives notifications when an entry has been removed from the cache

> There are several classes we are going to cover in this chapter that have an `@Beta` annotation indicating that the functionality of the class may be subject to change in future releases of Guava.

With the introduction complete, let's get started.

MapMaker

The MapMaker class is found in the com.google.common.collect package. So why are we talking about the Collections class in this chapter? Shouldn't we have covered that class in *Chapter 4, Working with Collections*? Although we could have covered the MapMaker class in *Chapter 4, Working with Collections*, we are going to treat the MapMaker class as a provider of the most basic caching functionality. The MapMaker class uses the fluent interface API, allowing us to quickly construct ConcurrentHashMap. Let's look at the following example:

```
ConcurrentMap<String,Book> books = new
MapMaker().concurrencyLevel(2)
              .softValues()
              .makeMap();
```

Here we are creating ConcurrentMap with String keys and Book objects for the values (specified by the generics on the ConcurrentMap declaration). Our first method call, concurrencyLevel(), sets the amount of concurrent modifications we will allow in the map. We've also specified the softValues() method so the values from the map are each wrapped in a SoftReference object and may be garbage-collected if the memory becomes low. Other options we could have specified include weakKeys() and weakValues(), but there is no option for using softKeys(). When using WeakReferences or SoftReferences for either keys or values, if one is garbage-collected, the entire entry is removed from the map; partial entries are never exposed to the client.

Guava caches

Before we go into detail on CacheBuilders, and the usage of Guava caches in our code, some background information is in order. Guava has two base interfaces for caching: Cache and LoadingCache. The LoadingCache interface extends the Cache interface.

Cache

The Cache interface offers mapping from keys to values. But there are a few methods the Cache interface offers that makes them so much more than what basic HashMap has to offer. The traditional idiom for working with maps/caches is that we present a key, and if the cache contains a value for the key, that value is returned. Otherwise, a null value is returned if no mapping is found for the given key. To place values in a cache, we would make a method call such as the following:

```
put(key,value);
```

Here we are explicitly associating the key and value in the cache or map. The `Cache` interface in Guava has the traditional `put` method, but reading from the `Cache` has a self-loading idiom with this method:

```
V value = cache.get(key, Callable<? Extends V> value);
```

The previous method will retrieve the value if present; otherwise, it will extract the value from the `Callable` instance, associate the value with the key, and return the value. It gives us the ability to replace the procedure in the following pattern in one call:

```
value = cache.get(key);
if(value == null){
    value = someService.retrieveValue();
    cache.put(key,value);
}
```

The use of a `Callable` object implies that an asynchronous operation could have occurred. But what do we do if we don't need/want to execute an asynchronous task? We would use the `Callables` class from the `com.google.common.util.concurrent` package. `Callables` has one method for working with the `Callable` interface as shown in the following example:

```
Callable<String> value = Callables.returning("Foo");
```

In the preceding code, the `returning()` method will construct and return a `Callable` instance that will return the given value when the `get` method on the `Callable` instance is executed. So we can reimplement the previous example as follows:

```
cache.get(key,Callables.returning(someService.retrieveValue()));
```

Keep in mind that if the value is already present, the cached value is returned. If we prefer the *retrieve if available, null otherwise* idiom, we have the `getIfPresent(key)` method that behaves in a more traditional manner. There are also methods to invalidate values in the cache. They are as follows:

- `invalidate(key)`: This method discards any value stored for this key
- `invalidateAll()`: This method discards all the values for the cache
- `invalidateAll(Iterable<?> keys)`: This method discards all the values for the given keys

LoadingCache

The `LoadingCache` interface extends the `Cache` interface with the self-loading functionality. Consider the following example:

```
Book book = loadingCache.get(id);
```

In the preceding code, if the `book` object was not available when the `get` call was executed, `LoadingCache` will know how to retrieve the object, store it in the cache, and return the value.

Loading values

As implementations of `LoadingCache` are expected to be thread safe, a call made to `get`, with the same key, while the cache is loading would block. Once the value was loaded, the call would return the value that was loaded by the original call to the `get` method. However, multiple calls to `get` with distinct keys will load concurrently. If we have a collection of keys and would like to retrieve the values for each key, we will make the following call:

```
ImmutableMap<key,value> map = cache.getAll(Iterable<? Extends
key>);
```

As we can see here, `getAll` returns `ImmutableMap` with the given keys and the values associated with those keys in the cache. The map returned from `getAll` could either be all cached values, all newly retrieved values, or a mix of already cached and newly retrieved values.

Refreshing values in the cache

`LoadingCache` also provides a mechanism for refreshing values in the cache:

```
refresh(key);
```

By making a call to `refresh`, `LoadingCache` will retrieve a new value for the key. The current value will not be discarded until the new value has been returned; this means that the calls to `get` during the loading process will return the current value in the cache. If an exception is thrown during the refresh call, the original value is kept in the cache. Keep in mind that if the value is retrieved asynchronously, the method could return before the value is actually refreshed.

CacheBuilder

The CacheBuilder class provides a way to obtain Cache and LoadingCache instances via the Builder pattern. There are many options we can specify on the Cache instance we are creating rather than listing all of them. Let's run through some examples so we can get a feel for how we can use caches in Guava. Our first example demonstrates how to specify invalidating a cache entry after loading it into the cache:

```
LoadingCache<String,TradeAccount> tradeAccountCache =
CacheBuilder.newBuilder()
                .expireAfterWrite(5L, TimeUnit.Minutes)
                .maximumSize(5000L)
                .removalListener(new
TradeAccountRemovalListener())
                .ticker(Ticker.systemTicker())
                .build(new CacheLoader<String, TradeAccount>() {
                    @Override
                    public TradeAccount load(String key) throws
Exception {
                        return
tradeAccountService.getTradeAccountById(key);
                    }
                });
```

Here we've constructed a LoadingCache for a TradeAccount object as shown in the following code:

```
public class TradeAccount {
    private String id;
    private String owner;
    private double balance;
}
```

Let's walk through our first example:

1. First, we called expireAfterWrite that will automatically remove the entry from the cache after the specified time, five minutes in this case.

2. Second, we specified the maximum size of the cache with the maximumSize call using 5000 as our value. Less recently used entries are subject to be removed as the size of the cache approaches the maximum size number, not necessarily when the actual maximum size is met or exceeded.

3. We added a `RemovalListener` instance that will receive notifications when an entry has been removed from the cache. `RemovalListener` will be covered later in this chapter.

4. We added a `Ticker` instance via the ticker method call that provides nanosecond-level precision for when entries should be expired.

5. Finally, we called the `build` method and passed a new `CacheLoader` instance that will be used to retrieve the `TradeAccount` objects when a key is presented to the cache and the value is not present.

In our next example, we look at how to invalidate cache entries based on how much time has elapsed since an entry was last accessed.

```
LoadingCache<String,Book> bookCache = CacheBuilder.newBuilder()
                .expireAfterAccess(20L,TimeUnit.MINUTES)
                .softValues()
                .removalListener(new BookRemovalListener())
                .build(new CacheLoader<String, Book>() {
                    @Override
                    public Book load(String key) throws Exception
{
                        return  bookService.getBookByIsbn(key);
                    }
                });
```

In this example, we are doing things slightly differently. Let's take a walk through this example:

1. We specify that we want entries to expire after 20 minutes have elapsed since a given entry was last accessed with the `expireAfterAccess` method call.

2. Instead of explicitly limiting the cache size to a certain value, we let the JVM limit the size implicitly by wrapping values in the cache with `SoftReferences` with a call to `softValues()`. When memory requirements are laid down, entries will be removed from the cache. Bear in mind that which `SoftReferences` are garbage-collected is determined by a least-recently-used (LRU) calculation on a JVM-wide scale.

3. Finally, we add the now familiar `RemovalListener` object and the a `CacheLoader` instance to retrieve absent values in the cache.

Now for our final example, we show how to automatically refresh values in the `loading` cache:

```
LoadingCache<String,TradeAccount> tradeAccountCache =
CacheBuilder.newBuilder()
                    .concurrencyLevel(10)
                    .refreshAfterWrite(5L,TimeUnit.SECONDS)
                    .ticker(Ticker.systemTicker())
                    .build(new CacheLoader<String,
TradeAccount>() {
                        @Override
                        public TradeAccount load(String key)
throws Exception {
                            return
tradeAccountService.getTradeAccountById(key);
                        }
                    });
```

In our final example, we have again made some small changes that are explained as follows:

1. We are providing guidelines for the amount of concurrent update operations with the `concurrencyLevel` method call with a value of `10`. If not explicitly set, the default value is `4`.

2. Instead of removing values explicitly, we are refreshing values after a given amount of time has passed. Note that the trigger for the refreshing values is activated when the value is requested and the time limit has expired.

3. We added the ticker for nanosecond precision for when values are eligible for a refresh.

4. Finally, we specified the loader to be used when calling the `build` method.

CacheBuilderSpec

The `CacheBuilderSpec` class can be used to create a `CacheBuilder` instance by parsing a string that represents the settings for `CacheBuilder`, (with the caveat that we lose compile time checking a malformed string that in turn will lead to a runtime error). Here's an example of a valid string used to create a `CacheBuilderSpec` instance:

```
String configString = "concurrencyLevel=10,refreshAfterWrite=5s"
```

This would create the same CacheBuilder instance we saw in the final example of CacheBuilder. For the options that specify the time (refreshAfterWrite, expireAfterAccess, and so on), the integer for the interval is followed by either of 's', 'm', 'h', or 'd', corresponding to seconds, minutes, hours, or days. There are no settings for milliseconds or nanoseconds. Once we have our configuration string, we can create an instance of the CacheBuilderSpec class as follows:

```
CacheBuilderSpec spec = CacheBuilderSpec.parse(configString);
```

We can then use the instance of the CacheBuilderSpec class to create a CacheBuilder instance:

```
CacheBuilder.from(spec);
```

Here we take the object of the CacheBuilderSpec class and call the static from method on the CacheBuilder class and return a CacheBuilder instance set with the properties from the formatted string. To add RemovalListener or to create LoadingCache from the builder, we use the returned CacheBuilder instance and make the appropriate method calls like we did before:

```
String spec =
"concurrencyLevel=10,expireAfterAccess=5m,softValues";
        CacheBuilderSpec cacheBuilderSpec =
CacheBuilderSpec.parse(spec);
        CacheBuilder cacheBuilder =
CacheBuilder.from(cacheBuilderSpec);
        cacheBuilder.ticker(Ticker.systemTicker())
            .removalListener(new TradeAccountRemovalListener())
            .build(new CacheLoader<String, TradeAccount>() {
                @Override
                public TradeAccount load(String key) throws
Exception {
                    return
tradeAccountService.getTradeAccountById(key);
                }
            });
```

Here we add a Ticker instance and a RemovalListener instance and specify CacheLoader to be used when calling the build method. Using a String literal for CacheBuilderSpec is for demonstration purposes only. Usually, this string would either be input from the command line or retrieved from a properties file.

CacheLoader

We have already seen `CacheLoader` in action by this point. But there are a few details we have not covered. The `CacheLoader` is an abstract class because of the fact that the `load` method is abstract. There is also a `loadAll` method that takes an `Iterable` object, but `loadAll` delegates this `Iterable` object to `load` for each item contained in the `Iterable` object (unless we've overridden the `loadAll` method). There are two static methods on the `CacheLoader` class that will allow us to leverage some of the constructs we have learned about from *Chapter 3, Functional Programming with Guava*. The first method is shown as follows:

```
CacheLoader<Key,value> cacheLoader =
CacheLoader.from(Function<Key,Value> func);
```

Here we can pass in a `Function` object that will transform an input object into an output object. When used as an argument of the `CacheLoader.from` method, we get a `CacheLoader` instance where the keys are the input objects to `Function` and the resulting output objects are the values. Similarly, we also have the second method shown as follows:

```
CacheLoader<Object,Value> cacheLoader =
CacheLoader.from(Supplier<Value> supplier);
```

In this preceding example, we are creating a `CacheLoader` instance from a `Supplier` instance. It's worth noting here that any key passed to `CacheLoader` will result in the `Supplier.get()` method being called. There is an implied assumption with both of these methods that we are re-using existing `Function` or `Supplier` instances and not creating new objects simply for the sake of creating `CacheLoader`.

CacheStats

Now that we've learned how to create a powerful caching mechanism, we are going to want to gather statistics on how our cache is performing and how it's being used. There is a very easy way to gather information on how our cache is performing. Keep in mind that tracking cache operations incurs a performance penalty. To gather statistics on our cache, we just need to specify that we want to record the statistics when using `CacheBuilder`:

```
LoadingCache<String,TradeAccount> tradeAccountCache =
CacheBuilder.newBuilder()
          .recordStats()
```

Here we are using a familiar pattern for constructing a `LoadingCache` instance. To enable the recording of statistics, all we need to do is add a `recordStats()` call on our builder. To read the performance statistics, all we need to do is call the `stats()` method on our `Cache/LoadingCache` instance, and we will get a reference to a `CacheStats` instance. Let's take the following example:

```
CacheStats cacheStats = cache.stats();
```

The following list is an overview of the type of information that can be obtained from the `CacheStats` class:

- The average time spent loading new values
- The fraction of requests to the cache that were hits
- The fraction of requests to the cache that were misses
- The number of evictions made by the cache

There is more information available on cache performance; what's listed previously is just a sample of the type of information available.

RemovalListener

We have seen in `CacheBuilder` examples of how we can add a `RemovalListener` instance to our cache. As the name implies, `RemovalListener` is notified when an entry is removed from the cache. As is the case with most listeners in Java, the `RemovalListener` is an interface and has one method, `onRemoval`, that takes a `RemovalNotification` object. `RemovalListener` is parameterized as follows:

```
RemovalListener<K,V>
```

Here, `K` is the type of the key we want to listen for and `V` is the type of the value we want to be notified of when removed. If we wanted to know about any entry being removed, we would simply use `Object` as the type parameter for both the key and value.

RemovalNotification

A `RemovalNotification` instance is the object the `RemovalListener` object receives when the removal of an entry is signaled. The `RemovalNotification` class implements the `Map.Entry` interface, and as a result, we can access the actual key and value objects that compose the entry in the cache. We should note that these values could be null if the entry was removed due to garbage collection.

We can also determine the reason for the removal by calling the getCause() method on the RemovalNotification instance that returns a RemovalCause enum. The possible values of the RemovalCause enum are as follows:

- COLLECTED: This value indicates that either the key or value were garbage-collected

- EXPIRED: This value indicates that the entry's last-written or last-accessed time limit has expired

- EXPLICIT: This value indicates that the user manually removed the entry

- REPLACED: This value indicates that the entry was not actually removed but the value was replaced

- SIZE: This value indicates that the entry was removed because the size of Cache approached or met the specified size limitation

If we need to perform any sort of operations when an entry is removed, it is best to do so asynchronously.

RemovalListeners

The RemovalListeners class facilitates how we can asynchronously process the removal notifications. To enable our RemovalListener instance to process any work triggered by the removal of an entry, we simply use the RemovalListeners. asynchronous method shown as follows:

```
RemovalListener<String,TradeAccount> myRemovalListener = new
RemovalListener<String, TradeAccount>() {
        @Override
        public void onRemoval(RemovalNotification<String,
TradeAccount> notification) {
              //Do something here
        }
    };
RemovalListener<String,TradeAccount> removalListener =
RemovalListeners.asynchronous(myRemovalListener,executorService);
```

Here we are taking previously constructed RemovalListener and ExecutorService, and passing them as arguments to the asynchronous method. We are returned a RemovalListener instance that will process removal notifications asynchronously. This step should occur before we register our RemovalListener object with the CacheBuilder instance.

Summary

In this chapter, we learned about the powerful Guava caching mechanisms. We saw how to create the simplest of caches by creating ConcurrentMap with the MapMaker class. Next, we learned about the advanced features of Cache and very powerful LoadingCache that will retrieve and cache values not present when requested. We explored CacheBuilder and discussed the many configuration options available, and how we can use CacheBuilder to configure the cache to suit our purposes. We discussed CacheLoader and learned how this powerful class is the muscle behind LoadingCache. We learned how to measure our cache performance through CacheStats class. Finally, we covered how to receive notifications of removed entries through the RemovalListener class. In the next chapter, we look at how to implement event-based programming by utilizing the EventBus class from Guava.

7
The EventBus Class

When developing software, the idea of objects sharing information or collaborating with each other is a must. The difficulty lies in ensuring that communication between objects is done effectively, but not at the cost of having highly coupled components. Objects are considered highly coupled when they have too much detail about other components' responsibilities. When we have high coupling in an application, maintenance becomes very challenging, as any change can have a rippling effect. To help us cope with this software design issue, we have event-based programming. In event-based programming, objects can either subscribe/listen for specific events, or publish events to be consumed. In Java, we have had the idea of event listeners for some time. An event listener is an object whose purpose is to be notified when a specific event occurs. We saw an example of an event listener, the `RemovalListener`, in *Chapter 6, Guava Cache*. In this chapter, we are going to discuss the Guava `EventBus` class and how it facilitates the publishing and subscribing of events. The `EventBus` class will allow us to achieve the level of collaboration we desire, while doing so in a manner that results in virtually no coupling between objects. It's worth noting that the `EventBus` is a lightweight, in-process publish/subscribe style of communication, and is not meant for inter-process communication.

In this chapter, we are going to cover the following things:

- The `EventBus` and `AsyncEventBus` classes
- Subscribing to events and registering with `EventBus` to be notified of events
- Publishing events with `EventBus`
- Writing event handlers and choosing between coarse-grained or fine-grained event handlers depending on our needs
- Using a dependency injection framework in conjunction with `EventBus`

> We are going to cover several classes in this chapter that have an @Beta annotation indicating that the functionality of the class may be subject to change in future releases of Guava.

EventBus

The EventBus class (found in the com.google.common.eventbus package) is the focal point for establishing the publish/subscribe-programming paradigm with Guava. At a very high level, subscribers will register with EventBus to be notified of particular events, and publishers will send events to EventBus for distribution to interested subscribers. All the subscribers are notified serially, so it's important that any code performed in the event-handling method executes quickly.

Creating an EventBus instance

Creating an EventBus instance is accomplished by merely making a call to the EventBus constructor:

```
EventBus eventBus = new EventBus();
```

We could also provide an optional string argument to create an identifier (for logging purposes) for EventBus:

```
EventBus eventBus = new EventBus(TradeAccountEvent.class.getName());
```

Subscribing to events

The following three steps are required by an object to receive notifications from EventBus,:

1. The object needs to define a public method that accepts only one argument. The argument should be of the event type for which the object is interested in receiving notifications.

2. The method exposed for an event notification is annotated with an @Subscribe annotation.

3. Finally, the object registers with an instance of EventBus, passing itself as an argument to the EventBus.register method.

Posting the events

To post an event, we need to pass an event object to the `EventBus.post` method. `EventBus` will call the registered subscriber handler methods, taking arguments that are assignable to the event object type. This is a very powerful concept because interfaces, superclasses, and interfaces implemented by superclasses are included, meaning we can easily make our event handlers as course- or fine-grained as we want, simply by changing the type accepted by the event-handling method.

Defining handler methods

Methods used as event handlers must accept only one argument, the event object. As mentioned before, `EventBus` will call event-handling methods serially, so it's important that those methods complete quickly. If any extended processing needs to be done as a result of receiving an event, it's best to run that code in a separate thread.

Concurrency

`EventBus` will not call the handler methods from multiple threads, unless the handler method is marked with the `@AllowConcurrentEvent` annotation. By marking a handler method with the `@AllowConcurrentEvent` annotation, we are asserting that our handler method is thread-safe. Annotating a handler method with the `@AllowConcurrentEvent` annotation by itself will not register a method with `EventBus`.

Now that we have defined how we can use `EventBus`, let's look at some examples.

Subscribe – An example

Let's assume we have defined the following `TradeAccountEvent` class as follows:

```
public class TradeAccountEvent {

    private double amount;
    private Date tradeExecutionTime;
    private TradeType tradeType;
    private TradeAccount tradeAccount;

    public TradeAccountEvent(TradeAccount account, double amount,
Date tradeExecutionTime, TradeType tradeType) {
        checkArgument(amount > 0.0, "Trade can't be less than
zero");
```

```
        this.amount = amount;
        this.tradeExecutionTime =
checkNotNull(tradeExecutionTime,"ExecutionTime can't be null");
        this.tradeAccount = checkNotNull(account,"Account can't be
null");
        this.tradeType = checkNotNull(tradeType,"TradeType can't
be null");
    }
//Details left out for clarity
```

So whenever a buy or sell transaction is executed, we will create an instance of the TradeAccountEvent class. Now let's assume we have a need to audit the trades as they are being executed, so we have the SimpleTradeAuditor class as follows:

```
public class SimpleTradeAuditor {

    private List<TradeAccountEvent> tradeEvents =
Lists.newArrayList();

    public SimpleTradeAuditor(EventBus eventBus){
        eventBus.register(this);
    }

    @Subscribe
    public void auditTrade(TradeAccountEvent tradeAccountEvent){
        tradeEvents.add(tradeAccountEvent);
        System.out.println("Received trade "+tradeAccountEvent);
    }
}
```

Let's quickly walk through what is happening here. In the constructor, we are receiving an instance of an EventBus class and immediately register the SimpleTradeAuditor class with the EventBus instance to receive notifications on TradeAccountEvents. We have designated auditTrade as the event-handling method by placing the @Subscribe annotation on the method. In this case, we are simply adding the TradeAccountEvent object to a list and printing out to the console acknowledgement that we received the trade.

Event Publishing – An example

Now let's take a look at a simple event publishing example. For executing our trades, we have the following class:

```
public class SimpleTradeExecutor {

    private EventBus eventBus;

    public SimpleTradeExecutor(EventBus eventBus) {
        this.eventBus = eventBus;
    }

    public void executeTrade(TradeAccount tradeAccount, double
amount, TradeType tradeType){
        TradeAccountEvent tradeAccountEvent =
processTrade(tradeAccount, amount, tradeType);
        eventBus.post(tradeAccountEvent);
    }

    private TradeAccountEvent processTrade(TradeAccount
tradeAccount, double amount, TradeType tradeType){
        Date executionTime = new Date();
        String message = String.format("Processed trade for %s of
amount %n type %s @
%s",tradeAccount,amount,tradeType,executionTime);
        TradeAccountEvent tradeAccountEvent = new TradeAccountEvent(tr
adeAccount,amount,executionTime,tradeType);
        System.out.println(message);
        return tradeAccountEvent;
    }
}
```

Like the `SimpleTradeAuditor` class, we are taking an instance of the `EventBus` class in the `SimpleTradeExecutor` constructor. But unlike the `SimpleTradeAuditor` class, we are storing a reference to the `EventBus` for later use. While this may seem obvious to most, it is critical for the same instance to be passed to both classes. We will see in future examples how to use multiple `EventBus` instances, but in this case, we are using a single instance. Our `SimpleTradeExecutor` class has one public method, `executeTrade`, which accepts all of the required information to process a trade in our simple example. In this case, we call the `processTrade` method, passing along the required information and printing to the console that our trade was executed, then returning a `TradeAccountEvent` instance. Once the `processTrade` method completes, we make a call to `EventBus.post` with the returned `TradeAccountEvent` instance, which will notify any subscribers of the `TradeAccountEvent` object. If we take a quick view of both our publishing and subscribing examples, we see that although both classes participate in the sharing of required information, neither has any knowledge of the other.

Finer-grained subscribing

We have just seen examples on publishing and subscribing using the `EventBus` class. If we recall, `EventBus` publishes events based on the type accepted by the subscribed method. This gives us some flexibility to send events to different subscribers by type. For example, let's say we want to audit the buy and sell trades separately. First, let's create two separate types of events:

```
public class SellEvent extends TradeAccountEvent {

    public SellEvent(TradeAccount tradeAccount, double amount, Date
tradExecutionTime) {
        super(tradeAccount, amount, tradExecutionTime, TradeType.
SELL);
    }
}


public class BuyEvent extends TradeAccountEvent {

    public BuyEvent(TradeAccount tradeAccount, double amount, Date
tradExecutionTime) {
        super(tradeAccount, amount, tradExecutionTime, TradeType.BUY);
    }
}
```

Now we have created two discrete event classes, `SellEvent` and `BuyEvent`, both of which extend the `TradeAccountEvent` class. To enable separate auditing, we will first create a class for auditing `SellEvent` instances:

```java
public class TradeSellAuditor {

    private List<SellEvent> sellEvents = Lists.newArrayList();

    public TradeSellAuditor(EventBus eventBus) {
        eventBus.register(this);
    }

    @Subscribe
    public void auditSell(SellEvent sellEvent){
        sellEvents.add(sellEvent);
        System.out.println("Received SellEvent "+sellEvent);
    }

    public List<SellEvent> getSellEvents() {
        return sellEvents;
    }
}
```

Here we see functionality that is very similar to the `SimpleTradeAuditor` class with the exception that this class will only receive the `SellEvent` instances. Then we will create a class for auditing only the `BuyEvent` instances:

```java
public class TradeBuyAuditor {

    private List<BuyEvent> buyEvents = Lists.newArrayList();

    public TradeBuyAuditor(EventBus eventBus) {
        eventBus.register(this);
    }

    @Subscribe
    public void auditBuy(BuyEvent buyEvent){
        buyEvents.add(buyEvent);
        System.out.println("Received TradeBuyEvent "+buyEvent);
    }

    public List<BuyEvent> getBuyEvents() {
        return buyEvents;
    }
}
```

Now we just need to refactor our `SimpleTradeExecutor` class to create the correct `TradeAccountEvent` instance class based on whether it's a buy or sell transaction:

```
public class BuySellTradeExecutor {
    ... deatails left out for clarity same as SimpleTradeExecutor
//The executeTrade() method is unchanged from SimpleTradeExecutor

    private TradeAccountEvent processTrade(TradeAccount tradeAccount,
double amount, TradeType tradeType) {
        Date executionTime = new Date();
        String message = String.format("Processed trade for %s of
amount %n type %s @ %s", tradeAccount, amount, tradeType,
executionTime);
        TradeAccountEvent tradeAccountEvent;
        if (tradeType.equals(TradeType.BUY)) {
            tradeAccountEvent = new BuyEvent(tradeAccount, amount,
executionTime);

        } else {
            tradeAccountEvent = new SellEvent(tradeAccount,
amount, executionTime);
        }
        System.out.println(message);
        return tradeAccountEvent;
    }
}
```

Here we've created a new `BuySellTradeExecutor` class that behaves in the exact same manner as our `SimpleTradeExecutor` class, with the exception that depending on the type of transaction, we create either a `BuyEvent` or `SellEvent` instance. However, the `EventBus` class is completely unaware of any of these changes. We have registered different subscribers and we are posting different events, but these changes are transparent to the `EventBus` instance. Also, take note that we did not have to create separate classes for the notification of events. Our `SimpleTradeAuditor` class would have continued to receive the events as they occurred. If we wanted to do separate processing depending on the type of event, we could simply add a check for the type of event. Finally, if needed, we could also have a class that has multiple subscribe methods defined:

```
public class AllTradesAuditor {

    private List<BuyEvent> buyEvents = Lists.newArrayList();
    private List<SellEvent> sellEvents = Lists.newArrayList();
```

```java
    public AllTradesAuditor(EventBus eventBus) {
        eventBus.register(this);
    }

    @Subscribe
    public void auditSell(SellEvent sellEvent){
        sellEvents.add(sellEvent);
        System.out.println("Received TradeSellEvent "+sellEvent);
    }

    @Subscribe
    public void auditBuy(BuyEvent buyEvent){
        buyEvents.add(buyEvent);
        System.out.println("Received TradeBuyEvent "+buyEvent);
    }

}
```

Here we've created a class with two event-handling methods. The `AllTradesAuditor` method will receive notifications about all trade events; it's just a matter of which method gets called by `EventBus` depending on the type of event. Taken to an extreme, we could create an event handling method that accepts a type of `Object`, as `Object` is an actual class (the base class for all other objects in Java), and we could receive notifications on any and all events processed by `EventBus`. Finally, there is nothing preventing us from having more than one `EventBus` instance. If we were to refactor the `BuySellTradeExecutor` class into two separate classes, we could inject a separate `EventBus` instance into each class. Then it would be a matter of injecting the correct `EventBus` instance into the auditing classes, and we could have complete event publishing-subscribing independence. We won't show an example here, but the reader should consult the sample code found in the `bbejeck.guava.chapter7.config` package to see how that would work.

Unsubscribing to events

Just as we want to subscribe to events, it may be desirable at some point to turn off the receiving of events. This is accomplished by passing the subscribed object to the `eventBus.unregister` method. For example, if we know at some point that we would want to stop processing events, we could add the following method to our subscribing class:

```java
public void unregister(){
        this.eventBus.unregister(this);
    }
```

Once this method is called, that particular instance will stop receiving events for whatever it had previously registered for. Other instances that are registered for the same event will continue to receive notifications.

AsyncEventBus

We stated earlier the importance of ensuring that our event-handling methods keep the processing light due to the fact that the EventBus processes all events in a serial fashion. However, we have another option with the AsyncEventBus class. The AsyncEventBus class offers the exact same functionality as the EventBus, but uses a provided java.util.concurrent.Executor instance to execute handler methods asynchronously.

Creating an AsyncEventBus instance

We create an AsyncEventBus instance in a manner similar to the EventBus instance:

```
AsyncEventBus asyncEventBus = new AsyncEventBus(executorService);
```

Here we are creating an AsyncEventBus instance by providing a previously created ExecutorService instance. We also have the option of providing a String identifier in addition to the ExecutorService instance. AsyncEventBus is very helpful to use in situations where we suspect the subscribers are performing heavy processing when events are received.

DeadEvents

When EventBus receives a notification of an event through the post method, and there are no registered subscribers, the event is wrapped in an instance of a DeadEvent class. Having a class that subscribes for DeadEvent instances can be very helpful when trying to ensure that all events have registered subscribers. The DeadEvent class exposes a getEvent method that can be used to inspect the original event that was undelivered. For example, we could provide a very simple class, which is shown as follows:

```
public class DeadEventSubscriber {

    private static final Logger logger =
Logger.getLogger(DeadEventSubscriber.class);

    public DeadEventSubscriber(EventBus eventBus) {
            eventBus.register(this);
```

```
    }

    @Subscribe
    public void handleUnsubscribedEvent(DeadEvent deadEvent){
        logger.warn("No subscribers for "+deadEvent.getEvent());
    }
}
```

Here we are simply registering for any DeadEvent instances and logging a warning for the original unclaimed event.

Dependency injection

To ensure we have registered our subscribers and publishers with the same instance of an EventBus class, using a dependency injection framework (Spring or Guice) makes a lot of sense. In the following example, we will show how to use the Spring Framework Java configuration with the SimpleTradeAuditor and SimpleTradeExecutor classes. First, we need to make the following changes to the SimpleTradeAuditor and SimpleTradeExecutor classes:

```
@Component
public class SimpleTradeExecutor {

    private EventBus eventBus;

    @Autowired
    public SimpleTradeExecutor(EventBus eventBus) {
        this.eventBus = checkNotNull(eventBus, "EventBus can't be
null");
    }

@Component
public class SimpleTradeAuditor {

    private List<TradeAccountEvent> tradeEvents =
Lists.newArrayList();

    @Autowired
    public SimpleTradeAuditor(EventBus eventBus){
        checkNotNull(eventBus,"EventBus can't be null");
        eventBus.register(this);
    }
```

Here we've simply added an @Component annotation at the class level for both the classes. This is done to enable Spring to pick these classes as **beans**, which we want to inject. In this case, we want to use constructor injection, so we added an @Autowired annotation to the constructor for each class. Having the @Autowired annotation tells Spring to inject an instance of an EventBus class into the constructor for both objects. Finally, we have our configuration class that instructs the Spring Framework where to look for components to wire up with the beans defined in the configuration class.

```
@Configuration
@ComponentScan(basePackages = {"bbejeck.guava.chapter7.publisher",
                               "bbejeck.guava.chapter7.subscriber"})
public class EventBusConfig {
    @Bean
    public EventBus eventBus() {
        return new EventBus();
    }
}
```

Here we have the @Configuration annotation, which identifies this class to Spring as a **Context** that contains the beans to be created and injected if need be. We defined the eventBus method that constructs and returns an instance of an EventBus class, which is injected into other objects. In this case, since we placed the @Autowired annotation on the constructors of the SimpleTradeAuditor and SimpleTradeExecutor classes, Spring will inject the same EventBus instance into both classes, which is exactly what we want to do. While a full discussion of how the Spring Framework functions is beyond the scope of this book, it is worth noting that Spring creates singletons by default, which is exactly what we want here. As we can see, using a dependency injection framework can go a long way in ensuring that our event-based system is configured properly. Consult the sample code found in the bbejeck.guava.chapter7.config package for another example showing how to configure more than one EventBus instance in an application.

Summary

In this chapter, we have covered how to use event-based programing to reduce coupling in our code by using the Guava EventBus class. We covered how to create an EventBus instance and register subscribers and publishers. We also explored the powerful concept of using types to register what events we are interested in receiving. We learned about the AsyncEventBus class, which allows us to dispatch events asynchronously. We saw how we can use the DeadEvent class to ensure we have subscribers for all of our events. Finally, we saw how we can use dependency injection to ease the setup of our event-based system. In the next chapter, we will take a look at working with files in Guava.

8
Working with Files

Reading from and writing to files is a core responsibility for programmers. Surprisingly enough, while Java has a rich and robust library for working in I/O, it's cumbersome to perform some basic tasks. While this has changed with the release of Java 7, users of Java 6 are still out of luck. Fortunately, Guava does what we've come to expect from this great library, giving us a set of tools to make working with I/O much easier. Even though Java 7 has introduced several improvements that address issues that Guava aimed to fix, we'll find that the tools provided to us make Guava I/O still very useful. We are going to learn about the following things in this chapter:

- Using the `Files` class to help with common tasks such as moving or copying files, or reading the lines of a file into a list of strings

- The `Closer` class, which gives us a very clean way of ensuring `Closeable` instances are properly closed

- The `ByteSource` and `CharSource` classes, which are immutable suppliers of input streams and readers

- The `ByteSink` and `CharSink` classes, which are immutable suppliers of output streams and writers

- The `CharStreams` and `ByteStreams` classes, which offer static utility methods for working with `Readers`, `Writers`, `InputStreams`, and `OutputStreams` classes respectively

- The `BaseEncoding` class, which offers methods for encoding and decoding byte sequences and ASCII characters

> There are several classes we are going to cover in this chapter that have an @Beta annotation indicating that the functionality of the class may be subject to change in the future releases of Guava.

Copying a file

The `Files` class offers several helpful methods for working with the `File` objects. For any Java developer, copying one file to another is a very challenging experience. But let's consider how we could accomplish the same task in Guava, using the `Files` class:

```
File original  = new File("path/to/original");
    File copy = new File("path/to/copy");
Files.copy(original, copy);
```

Moving/renaming a File

Moving files in Java is equally as cumbersome as copying. With Guava, moving a file is very easily achieved as shown in the following block of code:

```
public class GuavaMoveFileExample {

    public static void main(String[] args) {
        File original = new File("src/main/resources/copy.txt");
        File newFile = new File("src/main/resources/newFile.txt");
        try{
            Files.move(original, newFile);
        }catch (IOException e){
            e.printStackTrace();
        }
    }
}
```

In this example, we are taking the `copy.txt` file and re-naming it to `newFile.txt`. As we can see, it's as simple as calling the `Files.move` method.

Working with files as strings

There are times when we need to manipulate or work with files as strings. The `Files` class has methods for reading a file into a list of strings, returning the first line of a file as a string, and reading the contents of an entire file into a string. In our first example, we are going to show how to read a file into a list of strings by calling the `Files.readLines` method:

```
@Test
    public void readFileIntoListOfStringsTest() throws Exception{
        File file = new File("src/main/resources/lines.txt");
```

```
        List<String> expectedLines = Lists.newArrayList("The quick
brown","fox jumps over","the lazy dog");
        List<String> readLines = Files.readLines(file,
Charsets.UTF_8);
        assertThat(expectedLines,is(readLines));
    }
```

For this example, we are using a unit test to confirm that reading in a simple file with three lines gives us the expected results. All lines in the list have the terminal newline character stripped off, but any other white space is left intact. There is another version of `Files.readLines` method that takes the `LineProcessor` instance as an additional argument. Each line is fed to the `LineProcessor.processLine` method, which returns a boolean. Lines from the file will continue to be streamed to the `LineProcessor` instance until the file is exhausted or the `LineProcessor.processLine` method returns false. Consider, we have the following CSV file that contains information about books:

```
"Savage, Tom",Being A Great Cook,Acme Publishers,ISBN-
123456,29.99,1
"Smith, Jeff",Art is Fun,Acme Publishers,ISBN-456789,19.99,2
"Vandeley, Art",Be an Architect,Acme Publishers,ISBN-
234567,49.99,3
"Jones, Fred",History of Football,Acme Publishers,ISBN-
345678,24.99,4
"Timpton, Patty",Gardening My Way,Acme Publishers,ISBN-
4567891,34.99,5
```

We want to extract the title of the book from each row. To accomplish this task we have written the following implementation of the `LineProcessor` interface:

```
public class ToListLineProcessor implements
LineProcessor<List<String>>{

    private static final Splitter splitter = Splitter.on(",");
    private List<String> bookTitles = Lists.newArrayList();
    private static final int TITLE_INDEX = 1;

    @Override
    public List<String> getResult() {
        return bookTitles;
    }

    @Override
    @Override
```

```
    public boolean processLine(String line) throws IOException {
        bookTitles.add(Iterables.get(splitter.split(line),TITLE_
INDEX));
        return true;
    }
```

Here we are going to split each line on commas, take the title of the book, which is the second item and add it to `List<String>`. Notice we are using the `Iterables` class again, this time the static `Iterables.get` method, to retrieve the book title. We always return true, as we want to collect all the book titles from the file. Here's a unit test that confirms our `LineProcessor` instance extracts the correct information:

```
@Test
    public void readLinesWithProcessor() throws Exception {
        File file = new File("src/main/resources/books.csv");
        List<String> expectedLines = Lists.newArrayList("Being A Great
Cook","Art is Fun","Be an Architect","History of Football","Gardening
My Way");
        List<String> readLines = Files.readLines(file, Charsets.UTF_8,
new ToListLineProcessor());
        assertThat(expectedLines,is(readLines));
    }
```

In this example, we simply took all the input, but we could have just as easily only taken *n* number of lines or filtered the data on some criteria.

Hashing a file

Generating the hash code for a file is another example of a very simple task that seems to require too much boilerplate code when done in Java. Fortunately, the `Files` class has a `hash` method, as shown in the following block of code:

```
public class HashFileExample {

    public static void main(String[] args) throws IOException {
        File file = new File("src/main/resources/sampleTextFileOne.
txt");
        HashCode hashCode = Files.hash(file, Hashing.md5());
        System.out.println(hashCode);
    }
}
```

In the preceding example, to use the `Files.hash` method, we supply a `File` object and a `HashFunction` instance; in this case, we are using a hash function that implements the MD5 algorithm, and the method returns a `HashCode` object. Hash functions will be covered in the next chapter.

Writing to files

When working with input/output streams, there are several steps we have to follow, which are:

1. Opening the input/output stream.
2. Reading bytes into or out of the stream.
3. When done, ensure all resources are properly closed in a `finally` block.

When we have to repeat this process, over and over again, it is error prone and makes the code less clear and less maintainable. The `Files` class offers convenience methods for writing/appending to a file or reading the contents of a file into a byte array. Most of these become one-liners with the opening and closing of resources being taken care of for us.

Writing and appending

An example of writing and appending to a file is shown as follows:

```
@Test
    public void appendingWritingToFileTest() throws IOException {
        File file = new File("src/test/resources/quote.txt");
        file.deleteOnExit();

        String hamletQuoteStart = "To be, or not to be";
        Files.write(hamletQuoteStart,file, Charsets.UTF_8);
assertThat(Files.toString(file,Charsets.UTF_8),is(hamletQuoteStart));

        String hamletQuoteEnd = ",that is the question";
        Files.append(hamletQuoteEnd,file,Charsets.UTF_8);
        assertThat(Files.toString(file, Charsets.UTF_8),
is(hamletQuoteStart + hamletQuoteEnd));
        String overwrite = "Overwriting the file";
        Files.write(overwrite, file, Charsets.UTF_8);
        assertThat(Files.toString(file, Charsets.UTF_8),
is(overwrite));
    }
```

In this example, we have a unit test that does the following things:

1. Creating a file for testing, and ensuring the file is deleted when the JVM exits.
2. We use the `File.write` method to write a string to the file and confirm the write was successful.

3. We then use the `File.append` method to add another string and again confirm the expected result that the file contains the concatenation of our strings.

4. Finally, we use the `Files.write` method again to overwrite the file and confirm that we have indeed overwritten the file.

While this is certainly a simple example, notice that we wrote to a file three times and we never once had to open or close any resources. As a result, our code becomes much easier to read and more importantly, less error prone.

InputSupplier and OutputSupplier

Guava has `InputSupplier` and `OutputSupplier` interfaces that are used as suppliers of `InputStreams`/`Readers` or `OutputStreams`/`Writers`. We'll see in the following section how these interfaces benefit us, as Guava will typically open, flush, and close the underlying resources when these interfaces are used.

Sources and Sinks

Guava I/O has the notion of Sources and Sinks for reading and writing files, respectively. Sources and Sinks are not streams', readers', or writers' objects themselves, but are also providers for the same. Source and Sink objects can be used in two ways:

- We can retrieve the underlying stream from the provider. Each time the provider returns a stream, it is a completely new instance, and independent from any others that may have been returned. Callers retrieving the underlying stream objects are responsible for closing the stream.

- There are basic convenience methods for performing basic operations we would expect, such as reading from a stream or writing to a stream. When performing reads and writes through the Sinks or Sources, the opening and closing of the streams are handled for us. Each operation involves opening and closing a new stream.

There are two types of Sources: `ByteSource` and `CharsSource`. Likewise, there are two types of Sinks: `ByteSink` and `CharSink`. The respective Source and Sink classes offer similar functionality, the differences in the methods are due to the fact that we are either working with characters or raw bytes. The `Files` class offers several of the methods offered by the `ByteSink` and `CharSink` classes that work on files. We can create a `ByteSource`, `ByteSink`, `CharSource`, or `CharSink` instance from static factory methods on the `Files` class, or the `ByteStreams` and `CharStreams` classes. In our examples, we are going to focus on `ByteSource` and `ByteSink` objects, but the `CharSource` and `CharSink` objects work in a similar fashion, just with characters.

ByteSource

A `ByteSource` class represents a readable source of bytes. Typically, we would expect the underlying source of the bytes to be from a file, but it could be from a byte array.

We can create `ByteSource` from a file object by using a static method from the `Files` class:

```
@Test
    public void createByteSourceFromFileTest() throws Exception {
        File f1 = new File("src/main/resources/sample.pdf");
        byteSource = Files.asByteSource(f1);
        byte[] readBytes = byteSource.read();
        assertThat(readBytes,is(Files.toByteArray(f1)));
    }
```

In this example, we are creating `ByteSource` from a file using the `Files.asByteSource` method. Next, we are demonstrating how we can read the contents of `ByteSource` into a byte array by calling the `read` method. Finally, we are asserting that the byte array returned from the `read` method is the same as the byte array returned from the `Files.toByteArray` method.

ByteSink

A `ByteSink` class represents a writable source of bytes. We can write the bytes to a file or the destination could be another byte array. To create `ByteSink` from a file, we would do the following:

```
@Test
    public void testCreateFileByteSink() throws Exception {
        File dest = new File("src/test/resources/byteSink.pdf");
        dest.deleteOnExit();
        byteSink = Files.asByteSink(dest);
        File file = new File("src/main/resources/sample.pdf");
        byteSink.write(Files.toByteArray(file));
        assertThat(Files.toByteArray(dest),is(Files.
toByteArray(file)));
    }
```

Here we are creating a `file` object, then calling the static `Files.asByteSink` method with the newly created `file` object as an argument. We then call the `write` method writing the bytes to their ultimate destination. Finally, we are asserting that the file contains our expected content. There is also a method on the `ByteSink` class where we can write to an `OutputStream` object.

Copying from a ByteSource class to a ByteSink class

Now we will tie the ByteSource and ByteSink classes together by showing an example of copying the underlying bytes from the ByteSource instance to a ByteSink instance. While this might seem obvious, there are some powerful concepts at work here. First, we are dealing at an abstract level with ByteSource and ByteSink instances; we really don't need to know the original sources for each. Second, the entire opening and closing of resources is handled for us.

```
@Test
    public void copyToByteSinkTest() throws Exception {
        File dest = new
File("src/test/resources/sampleCompany.pdf");
        dest.deleteOnExit();
        File source = new File("src/main/resources/sample.pdf");
        ByteSource byteSource = Files.asByteSource(source);
        ByteSink byteSink = Files.asByteSink(dest);
        byteSource.copyTo(byteSink);
        assertThat(Files.toByteArray(dest),
is(Files.toByteArray(source)));
    }
```

Here we are creating a ByteSource instance and a ByteSink instance using the familiar static methods from the Files class. We are then calling the ByteSource. copyTo method writing the bytes to the byteSink object. Then we verify that the contents of our new file match the contents of our source file. The ByteSink class also has a copyTo() method that takes OutputStream as the destination to copy the bytes to.

ByteStreams and CharStreams

ByteStreams is a utility class for working with InputStream and OutputStream instances, and the CharStreams class is a utility class for working with Reader and Writer instances. Several of the methods offered by the ByteStreams and CharStreams classes that operate directly on files are also offered in the Files class. Several of the methods operate by copying the entire contents of a stream or reader to another OutputSupplier, OutputStream, or Writer instance. There are too many methods to go into detail here, so we will instead go over a couple of interesting methods found in each class.

Limiting the size of InputStreams

The ByteSteams.limit method takes InputStream and a long value and returns a wrapped InputStream that will only read the number of bytes equal to the long value given. Let's take a look at an example:

```
@Test
    public void limitByteStreamTest() throws Exception {
        File binaryFile = new
File("src/main/resources/sample.pdf");
        BufferedInputStream inputStream = new
BufferedInputStream(new FileInputStream(binaryFile));
        InputStream limitedInputStream =
ByteStreams.limit(inputStream,10);
        assertThat(limitedInputStream.available(),is(10));
        assertThat(inputStream.available(),is(218882));
    }
```

In this example, we are creating InputStream for one of our sample files, sample.pdf. We are then creating InputStream that will be limited to 10 bytes from the underlying stream via the ByteStreams.limit method. We then verify whether our new *limited* InputStream is correct by asserting the number of available bytes to read is 10, and we also assert that the size of the original stream is much higher.

Joining CharStreams

The CharStreams.join method takes multiple InputSupplier instances and joins them so that they logically appear as one InputSupplier instance, and writes out their contents to an OutputSupplier instance:

```
@Test
    public void joinTest() throws Exception {
        File f1 = new
File("src/main/resources/sampleTextFileOne.txt");
        File f2 = new
File("src/main/resources/sampleTextFileTwo.txt");
        File f3 = new File("src/main/resources/lines.txt");
        File joinedOutput = new
File("src/test/resources/joined.txt");
        joinedOutput.deleteOnExit();

        List<InputSupplier<InputStreamReader>> inputSuppliers() =
getInputSuppliers()(f1,f2,f3);
```

```
        InputSupplier<Reader> joinedSupplier =
CharStreams.join(inputSuppliers());
        OutputSupplier<OutputStreamWriter> outputSupplier =
Files.newWriterSupplier(joinedOutput, Charsets.UTF_8);
        String expectedOutputString = joinFiles(f1,f2,f3);

        CharStreams.copy(joinedSupplier,outputSupplier);
        String joinedOutputString  = joinFiles(joinedOutput);
        assertThat(joinedOutputString,is(expectedOutputString));
    }
private String joinFiles(File ...files) throws IOException {
        StringBuilder builder = new StringBuilder();
        for (File file : files) {
            builder.append(Files.toString(file,Charsets.UTF_8));
        }
        return builder.toString();
    }


    private List<InputSupplier<InputStreamReader>>
getInputSuppliers()(File ...files){
        List<InputSupplier<InputStreamReader>> list  =
Lists.newArrayList();
        for (File file : files) {
            list.add(Files.newReaderSupplier(file,Charsets.UTF_8));
        }
        return list;
    }
```

This is a big example, so let's step through what we're doing here:

1. We are creating four File objects, three that are our source files that need to be joined, and an output file.

2. We use a private utility method on our test, getInputSuppliers(), that uses the Files.newReaderSupplier static factory method to create InputSupplier objects for each of our source files.

3. We then create InputSupplier that joins our list of InputSupplier instances into one logical InputSupplier.

4. We create OutputSupplier by calling the Files.newWriterSupplier factory method using the fourth file object we created in step one.

5. We use another private helper method, joinFiles, that calls the Files.toString method on each of the source files to create the expected value for our test.

6. We call the `CharStreams.copy` method that will write the contents of each of the underlying `InputSuppliers()` to `OutputSupplier`.

7. We verify whether the destination file contains the same content as the three original source files.

Closer

The `Closer` class in Guava is used to ensure that all the registered `Closeable` objects are properly closed when the `Closer.close` method is called. The `Closer` class emulates the behavior found with Java 7's try-with-resources idiom, but can be used in a Java 6 environment. Using the `Closer` class is straightforward and is done in the following manner:

```
public class CloserExample {

    public static void main(String[] args) throws IOException {
        Closer closer = Closer.create();
        try {
            File destination = new File("src/main/resources/copy.
txt");
            destination.deleteOnExit();

            BufferedReader reader = new BufferedReader(new
FileReader("src/main/resources/sampleTextFileOne.txt"));
            BufferedWriter writer = new BufferedWriter(new
FileWriter(destination));
            closer.register(reader);
            closer.register(writer);

            String line;
            while((line = reader.readLine())!=null){
                writer.write(line);
            }

        } catch (Throwable t) {
            throw closer.rethrow(t);
        } finally {
            closer.close();
        }
    }
}
```

In this example, we are simply setting up to copy a text file. First, we create an instance of a Closer class. Then we create BufferedReader and BufferedWriter, and then register those objects with the previously created Closer instance. We should mention here that all of the methods that use the InputSupplier and OutputSupplier instances use the Closer class to manage the closing of the underlying I/O resources, and in the opinion of the writer, it's better to use the Sources and Sinks objects covered previously than raw I/O streams, readers, or writers.

BaseEncoding

When dealing with binary data, we sometimes have a need to convert the bytes representing the data into printable ASCII characters. Of course, we also need to be able to convert the encoded bytes back into their raw decoded form. BaseEncoding is an abstract class that contains static factory methods for creating instances of different encoding schemes. In its simplest form, we can use the BaseEncoding class as follows:

```
@Test
    public void encodeDecodeTest() throws Exception {
        File file = new File("src/main/resources/sample.pdf");
        byte[] bytes = Files.toByteArray(file);
        BaseEncoding baseEncoding = BaseEncoding.base64();
        String encoded = baseEncoding.encode(bytes);
        assertThat(Pattern.matches("[A-Za-z0-
9+/=]+",encoded),is(true));
        assertThat(baseEncoding.decode(encoded),is(bytes));
    }
```

Here we are taking a binary file (a PDF document) and encoding the bytes to a base64 encoded string. We assert the string is composed entirely of ASCII characters. Then we convert the encoded string back to bytes and assert those are equal to the bytes we started with. But the BaseEncoding class gives us much more flexibility and power than simply encoding and decoding byte arrays. We can wrap the OutputSuplier, ByteSink, and Writer instances so that the bytes are encoded as they are written. Conversely, we can also wrap the IntputStream, ByteSource, and Reader instances that decode strings on the fly. Let's look at the following example:

```
@Test
    public void encodeByteSinkTest()  throws Exception{
        File file = new File("src/main/resources/sample.pdf");
        File encodedFile = new
File("src/main/resources/encoded.txt");
```

```
        encodedFile.deleteOnExit();
        CharSink charSink = Files.asCharSink(encodedFile,
Charsets.UTF_8);

        BaseEncoding baseEncoding = BaseEncoding.base64();
        ByteSink byteSink = baseEncoding.encodingSink(charSink);
        ByteSource byteSource = Files.asByteSource(file);
        byteSource.copyTo(byteSink);

        String encodedBytes = baseEncoding.encode(byteSource.read());
        assertThat(encodedBytes,is(Files.
toString(encodedFile,Charsets.UTF
_8)));
    }
```

In this example, we are creating two file objects, one representing our binary file and the other, the location where we are going to copy the original file. We next create a CharSink instance with our destination file object. Next, we create a BaseEncoding instance that will encode/decode using the base64 algorithm. We use the BaseEncoding instance to wrap our previously constructed CharSink in ByteSink so that bytes are automatically encoded as they are written. We are then creating ByteSource from our destination file and copying the bytes to our ByteSink. We then assert that the encoded bytes from our original file match the destination file when converted to a string.

Summary

We learned how Guava handles the opening and closing of our I/O resources when using InputSupplier and OutputSupplier. We also saw how to use the ByteSource, ByteSink, CharSource, and CharSink classes. Finally, we learned about the BaseEncoding class for converting binary data into text. In our next chapter, we wrap things up by covering the Hashing class and BloomFilter data structure, and avoiding null pointers with the Optional class.

9
Odds and Ends

We've reached the last chapter in this book but there is still so much to cover. While it's impossible to cover all of Guava in a book of this size, we've tried our best. This chapter is going to cover other useful tools from Guava that did not require an entire chapter by themselves. Also the ideas presented in this chapter might not need to be used everyday, but when you have the need, they can be indispensable. We are going to learn about the following things in this chapter:

- The `Hashing` class that contains static-utility methods for obtaining `HashFunction` instances

- The `BloomFilter` data structure that can be used to tell if an element is not present in a set. A `BloomFilter` data structure has the unique property that it can give a false positive about an element's presence but not a false negative about its absence

- The `Optional` class that gives us an alternative to using null references

- The `Throwables` class with static-utility methods for working with `Throwable` instances

Creating proper hash functions

Hash functions are fundamental in programming and are used for establishing identity and checking for duplicates. Also, they are essential for proper use of Java collections. Hash functions work by taking data of various lengths and mapping them to numbers. Since we are trying to map arbitrary data to numbers, it is essential that our hash function should be very resistant to collisions. In other words, we want to avoid generating the same numbers for different data. Needless to say, writing a good hash function is best left to the experts. Luckily, with Guava, we don't have to write our own hashing functions. The `Hashing` class provides static methods for creating `HashFunction` instances and there are a few types to be aware of.

Checksum hash functions

Guava provides two HashFunction classes that implement well-known checksum algorithms, Adler-32 and CRC-32. To create an instance of either HashFunction, we would do the following:

```
HashFunction adler32 = Hashing.adler32();
HashFunction crc32 = Hashing.crc32();
```

Here we are simply making a static method call the Hashing class to retrieve the desired HashFunction implementation.

General hash functions

Next we have what we'll call general hash functions. General hash functions are noncryptographic and are well suited to be used for hash-based lookup tasks. The first of these is the murmur hash, developed by *Austin Appleby* in 2008. The other general hash function is called goodFastHash. Let's take a look at creating the general hash functions:

```
HashFunction gfh = Hashing.goodFastHash(128);
HashFunction murmur3_32 = Hashing.murmur3_32();
HashFunction murmur3_128 = Hashing.murmur3_128();
```

The goodFastHash method returns the hash codes of a specified minimum number of bits in length, which is 128 in this case. Since there are 8 bits in a byte, the goodFastHash method call here would produce hash codes with a minimum length of 16 bytes (128 divided by 8) Next, we are creating two instances of the murmur hash. The first murmur hash instance is an implementation of the 32-bit murmur3_32 algorithm. The second murmur hash instance implements the 128-bit murmur3_128 hash algorithm.

> In the Guava documentation, the goodFastHash method has a warning that the implementation is subject to change.

Cryptographic hash functions

While a full description of a cryptographic hash function is beyond the scope of this book, we can say that cryptographic hash functions are used for information security. Generally speaking, cryptographic hash functions have the following properties:

- Any small change in the data results in a large change in the resulting hash code

- It is computationally infeasible that an attacker would be able to reverse engineer the hash code, that is, generate the message for a given hash code

There are three variants of cryptographic hash functions offered by Guava shown as follows:

```
HashFunction sha1 = Hashing.sha1();
HashFunction sha256 = Hashing.sha256();
HashFunction sha512 = Hashing.sha512();
```

The three hash functions we just saw implement the `sha-1`, `sha-256`, and `sha-512` hashing algorithms.

BloomFilter

Bloomfilters are a unique data structure used to indicate whether an element is contained in a set. What makes `BloomFilter` interesting is that it will indicate whether an element is *absolutely not* contained or *may be* contained in a set. This property of never having a false negative makes `BloomFilter` a great candidate for use as a guard condition to help prevent performing unnecessary or expensive operations, such as disk retrievals.

BloomFilter in a nutshell

Bloomfilter are essentially bit vectors. At a high level, Bloomfilter work in the following manner:

1. Add an element to the filter.

2. Hash it a few times and then set the bits to 1, where the index matches the results of the hash.

When testing whether an element is in the set, you follow the same hashing procedure and check whether the bits are set to 1 or 0. This process is about how `BloomFilter` can guarantee that an element is not present. If the bits aren't set, it's simply impossible for the element to be in the set. However, a positive answer means the element is in the set or a hashing collision has occurred. Before we cover creating and using Bloom filters in Guava, we need to talk about how we get the bytes from objects read into `BloomFilter` for hashing.

Funnels and PrimitiveSinks

The `Funnel` interface accepts objects of a certain type and sends data to a `PrimitiveSink` instance. `PrimitiveSink` is an object that receives primitive values. A `PrimitiveSink` instance will extract the bytes needed for hashing. A `Funnel` interface is used by `BloomFilter` to extract the bytes from the items placed in the `BloomFilter` data structure for hashing. Let's look at an example:

```
public enum BookFunnel implements Funnel<Book> {
    //This is the single enum value
    FUNNEL;
    public void funnel(Book from, PrimitiveSink into) {
        into.putBytes(from.getIsbn().getBytes(Charsets.UTF_8))
            .putDouble(from.getPrice());
    }
}
```

Here we are creating a simple `Funnel` instance that expects to receive `Book` instances. Note that we are implementing our `Funnel` as an enum, which helps maintain the serialization of `BloomFilter`, which also needs the `Funnel` instance to be serializable. The `ISBN` property (as a byte array) from `Book` and `Price` (double data types) are put into the `PrimitiveSink` instance and will be used to create the hash code representing the `Book` instance that is passed in.

Creating a BloomFilter instance

Now that we've seen how to create a `Funnel` instance, we are ready to create our `BloomFilter` instance:

```
BloomFilter<Book> bloomFilter = BloomFilter.create(new
BookFunnel(), 5);
```

In this example, we are creating a `BloomFilter` instance by calling the static factory's `create` method, passing in a `Funnel` instance and an integer, which represents the number of expected inserts into `BloomFilter`. If the number of expected insertions is greatly exceeded, the number of false positives will rise sharply. Let's take a look at a sample `BloomFilter` instance:

```java
public class BloomFilterExample {

    public static void main(String[] args) throws Exception {
        File booksPipeDelimited = new
File("src/main/resources/books.data");

        List<Book> books = Files.readLines(booksPipeDelimited,
Charsets.UTF_8, new LineProcessor<List<Book>>() {
Splitter splitter = Splitter.on('|');
            List<Book> books = Lists.newArrayList();
            Book.Builder builder = new Book.Builder();

            public boolean processLine(String line) throws
IOException {
                List<String> parts =
Lists.newArrayList(splitter.split(line));
                builder.author(parts.get(0))
                        .title(parts.get(1))
                        .publisher(parts.get(2))
                        .isbn(parts.get(3))
                        .price(Double.parseDouble(parts.get(4)));
                books.add(builder.build());
                return true;
            }

            @Override
            public List<Book> getResult() {
                return books;
            }
        });

        BloomFilter<Book> bloomFilter = BloomFilter.create(new
BookFunnel(), 5);
```

```
        for (Book book : books) {
            bloomFilter.put(book);
        }

        Book newBook = new Book.Builder().title("Mountain
Climbing").build();
        Book book1 = books.get(0);
        System.out.println("book "+book1.getTitle()+" contained
"+bloomFilter.mightContain(book1));
        System.out.println("book "+newBook.getTitle()+" contained
"+bloomFilter.mightContain(newBook));
    }
```

Following are the results of our test:

```
Book [Being A Great Cook] contained true
Book [Mountain Climbing] contained false
```

In this example, we are reading in a pipe-delimited file and using the `Files.readLines` method in conjunction with a `LineProcessor` callback to convert each line from the file into a `Book` object. Each `Book` instance is added to a list and when the file has been fully processed, the list of books is returned. We then create a `BloomFilter` instance with the `BookFunnel` enum with an expected number of insertions of 5. We then add all of the books from the list into `BloomFilter`. Finally, we test `BloomFilter` by calling `mightContain` with a book that was added to `BloomFilter` and one that was not.

While we may not need to use `BloomFilter` on a daily basis, it's a very useful tool to have in our arsenal.

Optional

Dealing with null objects is painful. It's probably safe to say that many errors have been caused by assuming that objects returned by a method could not possibly be null, only to be unpleasantly surprised. To help with this situation, Guava has the `Optional` class. `Optional` is an immutable object that may or may not contain a reference to another object. If the `Optional` class contains the instance, it is considered **present**, and if it does not contain the instance, it is considered **absent**. A good use case for the `Optional` class is to have methods that return values which return `Optional` instead. That way we are forcing clients to consider the fact that the returned value may not be present, and we should take action accordingly.

Creating an Optional instance

The Optional class is abstract, and while we could extend Optional directly, there are static methods we can use to create an Optional instance. For example:

1. Optional.absent() returns an empty Optional instance.

2. Optional.of(T ref) returns an Optional instance that contains an object of type T.

3. In Optional.fromNullable(T ref), if ref is not null, it returns an Optional instance containing the reference, otherwise, an empty Optional instance.

4. In Optional.or(Supplier<T> supplier), if the reference is present then the reference is returned, otherwise, the result of Supplier.get is returned.

Let's take a look at a couple of simple examples:

```
@Test
    public void testOptionalOfInstance(){
        TradeAccount tradeAccount = new
TradeAccount.Builder().build();
        Optional<TradeAccount> tradeAccountOptional =
Optional.of(tradeAccount);
        assertThat(tradeAccountOptional.isPresent(),is(true));
    }
```

In the preceding unit test example, we are using the static Optional.of method that returns an Optional instance wrapping the given object. We confirm that our instance is available by asserting that the isPresent method returns true. Probably of more interest is using the Optional.fromNullable method shown as follows:

```
@Test(expected = IllegalStateException.class)
    public void testOptionalNull(){
        Optional<TradeAccount> tradeAccountOptional =
Optional.fromNullable(null);
        assertThat(tradeAccountOptional.isPresent(),is(false));
        tradeAccountOptional.get();
    }
```

In this unit test example, we are creating an `Optional` instance using the `fromNullable` static method. In this case, we are also returned an `Optional` instance, but this time we assert that the call to `isPresent` method returns false. Furthermore, we assert that an attempt to retrieve the wrapped object by calling `get` throws `IllegalStateException` due to the fact that there is no instance present. `Optional.fromNullable` is a great method for wrapping objects before returning them to callers. The true importance of the `Optional` class is that it signals a value is not guaranteed to be present, and it forces us to deal with that fact.

Throwables

The `Throwables` class contains static-utility methods for working with instances of `java.lang.Throwable`. Errors and exceptions in Java programs are inevitable. Sometimes it would be nice to have a utility to help with navigating large stack traces. The `Throwables` class offers us such help. We are going to look at two methods in particular, `Throwables.getCausalChain` and `Throwables.getRootCause`.

Getting the chain of Throwables

The `Throwables.getCausalChain` method returns a list of `Throwable` instances starting with the top level `Throwable` instance followed by the nested `Throwable` instances in the chain. This is best illustrated with an example:

```
@Test
    public void testGetCausalChain() {
        ExecutorService executor =
Executors.newSingleThreadExecutor();
        List<Throwable> throwables = null;
        Callable<FileInputStream> fileCallable = new
Callable<FileInputStream>() {
            @Override
            public FileInputStream call() throws Exception {
                return new FileInputStream("Bogus file");
            }
        };
        Future<FileInputStream> fisFuture =
executor.submit(fileCallable);
        try {
            fisFuture.get();
```

```
        } catch (Exception e) {
            throwables = Throwables.getCausalChain(e);
        }
        assertThat(throwables.get(0).getClass().
isAssignableFrom(Execution
Exception.class),is(true));
        assertThat(throwables.get(1).getClass().
isAssignableFrom(FileNotFo
undException.class),is(true));
        executor.shutdownNow();
    }
```

In this example, we are creating a `Callable` instance that is meant to return a `FileInputStream` object, but we are purposely going to cause a `FileNotFoundException`. We then submit our `Callable` instance to an `ExecutorService` and are returned with a `Future` reference. When we call the `Future.get` method, we fully expect an exception to be thrown, and we get the causal chain of the exception hierarchy as a list from the `Throwables.getCausalChain` method. Finally, we assert that the first `Throwable` instance in the list is an `ExecutionException` exception and the second is `FileNotFoundException`. With this list of the `Throwable` instances, we could conceivably filter the list looking for only the exceptions we want to examine.

Obtaining the Root Cause Throwable

The `Throwables.getRootCause` method takes a `Throwable` instance and returns the root cause of the exception hierarchy. Here's an example:

```
@Test
    public void testGetRootCause() throws Exception {
        ExecutorService executor =
Executors.newSingleThreadExecutor();
        Throwable cause = null;
        final String nullString = null;
        Callable<String> stringCallable = new Callable<String>() {
            @Override
            public String call() throws Exception {
                return nullString.substring(0,2);
            }
        };
```

```
        Future<String> stringFuture=
executor.submit(stringCallable);
        try {
            stringFuture.get();
        } catch (Exception e) {
            cause = Throwables.getRootCause(e);
        }
        assertThat(cause.getClass().isAssignableFrom(NullPointerExcep
tion.
class),is(true));
        executor.shutdownNow();
    }
```

Again we are using a Callable instance that will intentionally throw an exception, this time a NullPointerException. When we catch the exception thrown from calling the get method on our returned Future, stringFuture, we then call the Throwables.getRootCause method, and assign the returned innermost Throwable instance to our cause variable. We then assert that the root cause was indeed a NullPointerException. While these methods won't replace the practice of sifting through stack traces in log files, they give us the opportunity to save potentially valuable information we could use later.

Summary

In this chapter, we have covered some useful classes, which will probably not be used on an everyday basis but will serve us well when needed. First, we learned about the hash functions and the hashing utilities provided. Then we saw how those hash functions tie into a useful data structure called BloomFilter. We also learned about the Optional class, which can be useful in making our code more robust by avoiding unexpected null values. Finally, we learned about the Throwables class, which contains some useful methods for navigating exceptions thrown from our programs.

Index

Symbols

@AllowConcurrentEvent annotation 87
@Autowired annotation 96
@Beta annotation 60, 73
@Component annotation 96
@Subscribe annotation 86

A

acquire method 70
addToList method 61
apply method 28, 32
arbitrary comparable objects
  Ranges with 53, 54
ArrayListMultimap
  about 46
  creating, methods for 46-48
Ascii class method 17
assertThat statements 41
AsyncEventBus
  about 94
  instance, creating 94
AsyncFunction class 59, 67
AsyncFunction interface 69
  about 68
  applying 69
asynchronous method 83

B

BaseEncoding 108, 109
BaseEncoding class 97
beans 96
BiMap
  about 49

BiMap.forcePut method, using 49, 50
BiMap.inverse method, using 50
BiMap.forcePut method
  using 49, 50
BiMap.inverse method
  using 50
BloomFilter
  about 113
  creating 114-116
  Funnel interface 114
  in nutshell 113
  PrimitiveSinks 114
BloomFilter instance 111
book object 76
BuySellTradeExecutor class 92
ByteSink class
  about 97, 103, 104
  ByteSource class, copying from 104
byteSink object 104
ByteSource class
  about 97, 102, 103
  copying from, to ByteSink class 104
ByteStreams class 97, 104
ByteStreams.limit method 105

C

CacheBuilder class 73, 74, 77-79
CacheBuilderSpec class 73, 79, 80
Cache interface 74, 75
CacheLoader class 73, 81
CacheLoader.from method 81
CacheStats class 73, 81, 82
Callable instance 75, 120
CharMatcher class
  about 15

using 19, 20
Charsets class
about 17
using 17
CharSink class 97
CharSource class 97, 102
CharStreams
about 104
joining 105-107
CharStreams class 97
CharStreams.copy method 107
checkArgument (Boolean expression,
Object message) method 22
checkElementIndex (int index, int size,
Object message) method 22
checkNotNull (T object, Object message)
method 22
checkState (Boolean expression, Object
message) method 22
CityByPopulation comparator 56
Closer class
about 97
joining 107, 108
collections 39
com.google.common.collect package 39
Comparator parameter 41
compareTo method
about 53
implementing 24
ComposedPredicateSuplier class 36
concurrencyLevel() 74
Condition.signal() 60
Condition.signalAll() method 60

D

DeadEvents 94, 95
dependency injection 95, 96

E

emptyToNull method 18
enterWhen method 61
equals method 28
EventBus
about 86
concurrency 87
events, posting 87

events, subscribing to 86
handler methods, defining 87
instance, creating 86
EventBus.register method 86
event publishing
example 89, 90
events
posting 87
subscribing to 86
unsubscribing to 93
ExecutorService instance 63

F

file
appending to 101, 102
as strings 98-100
copying 98
hashing 100
moving 98
renaming 98
writing to 101, 102
FileInputStream object 119
Files.asByteSource method 103
Files class 97
Files.move method 98
Files.readLines method 99
Files.toByteArray method 103
FileWriter instance 13
Finer-grained subscribing 90-93
firstNonNull method 23
FluentIterable class
about 40, 41
FluentIterable.filter method, using 40, 41
FluentIterable.transform method, using 41
FluentIterable.filter method
using 40, 41
FluentIterable.from method 41
FluentIterable.from() method 41
FluentIterable instance 41
FluentIterable.transform method
using 41
forcePut method 50
forMap method 30
Function interface
about 5, 27-29
using, guidelines for 29

Functions class
about 27
Functions.compose method, using 30, 31
Functions.forMap method, using 30
using 29
Functions.compose method
using 30, 31
Functions.forMap method
using 30
Funnel interface 114
FutureCallback class 59
FutureCallback interface
about 65
using 65, 66
FutureFallback class 59
FutureFallback interface
about 68
applying 70
Future.get method 67, 119
Futures
about 69
Asynchronous Transforms 69
FutureFallbacks, applying 69
Futures.addCallback method 65, 69
Futures class 59

G

getCause() method 83
getEvent method 94
get method 35
goodFastHash method 112
Google Collections Library 5, 39
Google Guava. *See* also Guava
Google Guava
about 5
using, cases 6
Gradle
Guava, using with 8
greatestOf method 57
Guava
API docs 7
downloading 7
installing, steps for 7
strings with 16
using, with Gradle 7, 8
using, with Maven 7, 8

Guava caches
Cache interface 74
LoadingCache interface 76

H

H2 (embedded database) v1.3.170
URL 9
handler methods
defining 87
hashCode method 23
hash codes
generating 23
hash functions
checksum algorithms 112
creating 111
cryptographic hash function 113
general 112
Hashing class 111
HashMultimap 48

I

immutable collections
about 54
instances, creating 54
InputStreams
size, limiting 105
InputSupplier object 102, 106
invalidateAll(Iterable<?> keys) method 75
invalidateAll() method 75
invalidate(key) method 75
isNullOrEmpty method 18
isPresent method 117
Iterable instances 40
Iterable object 81
Iterables.contains method 41
Iterables.get method 100

J

java.util.concurrent.Executor instance 94
java.util.Date object 28
Joiner class 12, 13
JSR-305 8
JUnit v4.11
URL 9

L

LineProcessor callback 116
LineProcessor instance 99
LinkedHashMap instance 14
ListenableFuture.addListener method 63, 64
ListenableFuture class
  about 59, 63
  obtaining 64
ListenableFuture.get method 67
Lists
  about 42
  Lists.partition method, using 42
Lists.newArrayList() method 41
Lists.partition method
  using 42
LoadingCache interface
  about 74-76
  values in cache, refreshing 76
  values, loading 76
lookup.apply() method 31
Lucene v4.2
  URL 9

M

MapJoiner class 15
MapJoiner method 13
MapMaker class 73, 74
Maps
  about 44
  Maps.asMap method, using 45
  Maps.uniqueIndex method, using 45
  transforming 46
Maps.asMap method
  using 45
Maps.EntryTransformer interface 46
MapSplitter class 15, 16
Maps.toMap method 45
Maps.transformEntries method 46
Maps.uniqueIndex method
  using 45
Maven
  Guava, using with 7, 8
memoizeWithExpiration method 37
Monitor class
  about 59-61

access methods 62, 63
  best practices 62
Monitor.enterIf method 62
Monitor.enter method 62
Monitor.enterWhen method 63
Monitor.tryEnterIf method 63
Monitor.tryEnter method 63
Multimaps
  about 46
  ArrayListMultimap 46-48
  HashMultimap 48
murmur hash instance 112

N

newLinkedHashMap() method 14
notifyAll() method 60
NullPointerException error 12
nullsFirst method 56
nullToEmpty method 18
null values
  checking for 23

O

Object.toString() 12
onSuccess method 65
Optional class 111, 116
Optional.fromNullable method 117
optional instance
  about 116
  creating, steps for 117, 118
ordering
  about 55
  instance, creating 55
  maximum values, retrieving 57
  minimum values, retrieving 57
  null, accounting for 56
  sorting, reversing 55, 56
  sorting, secondary 56
Ordering.from method 55
Ordering.greatestOf method 57
OutputSupplier instance 102, 105

P

padStart method 18
permit 70

PopulationPredicate 33
Preconditions class
  using 20-22
Predicate interface
  about 27, 40
  example 32
  using 32
Predicates.and method
  using 33, 34
Predicates class
  about 27
  Predicates.and method, using 33, 34
  Predicates.compose method, using 34, 35
  Predicates.not method, using 34
  Predicates.or method, using 34
  using 33
Predicates.compose method
  about 33, 36, 53
  using 34, 35
Predicates.not method
  using 34
PrimitiveSink 114

R

Range
  about 52, 53
  with arbitrary comparable objects 53, 54
Range class 39
RateLimiter class 59, 70
recordStats() call 82
ReentrantLock class 60
RemovalCause enum
  COLLECTED 83
  EXPIRED 83
  EXPLICIT 83
  REPLACED 83
  SIZE 83
RemovalListener class
  about 73, 82, 83
  adding 80
  RemovalNotification class 82
  RemovalNotification instance 83
RemovalListeners.asynchronous method 83
RemovalNotification class 82
returning() method 75

S

Sets
  about 42, 43
  Sets.difference method, using 43
  Sets.intersection method, using 43
  Sets.symmetricDifference method, using 43
  Sets.union method, using 44
Sets.difference method
  using 43
Sets.intersection method
  using 43
Sets.symmetricDifference method
  using 43
Sets.union method
  using 44
SettableFuture class 59, 66, 67
SetView 43
SimpleDateFormat class 28
SimpleTradeExecutor class 92
SimpleTradeExecutor constructor 90
skipNulls class 12
SoftReferences 74, 78
softValues() method 74
source code
  getting 8, 9
Splitter class 14, 15
Splitter instance 15
Splitter object 16
Spring Java config Version 3.2
  URL 9
StandardCharsets class 17
stateFunction.apply() method 31
StringBuilder class 12, 13
StringBuilder instance 13
strings
  files, working with as 98
Strings class
  using 18
String.split method 14, 15
Supplier.get() method 81
Supplier interface
  about 5, 27
  example 35, 36
  using 35
Suppliers class
  about 27

Suppliers.memoize method, using 37
Suppliers.memoizeWithExpiration method,
    using 37
using 36
Suppliers.memoize method
  using 37
Suppliers.memoizeWithExpiration method
  using 37

T

Table
  about 50, 51
  operations 51
  views 52
threads
  synchronizing 60
Throwable object 66
Throwables
  about 118
  chain, getting 118, 119
  Root Cause Throwable, obtaining 119, 120
Throwables class 111
Throwables.getRootCause method 120
toMap method 41
toSet method 41
toSortedList method 41
toSortedSet method 41
toString method 22, 23
TradeAccountEvent instance 90
transform method 41
trimAndCollapseFrom method 19
trimResults method 15
tryAcquire method 70

U

UnsupportedEncodingException error 17
useForNull method 12
useForNull() method 13

W

withKeyValueSeparator method 13

[PACKT] open source ✼

PUBLISHING · community experience distilled

Thank you for buying
Getting Started with Google Guava

About Packt Publishing

Packt, pronounced 'packed', published its first book "*Mastering phpMyAdmin for Effective MySQL Management*" in April 2004 and subsequently continued to specialize in publishing highly focused books on specific technologies and solutions.

Our books and publications share the experiences of your fellow IT professionals in adapting and customizing today's systems, applications, and frameworks. Our solution based books give you the knowledge and power to customize the software and technologies you're using to get the job done. Packt books are more specific and less general than the IT books you have seen in the past. Our unique business model allows us to bring you more focused information, giving you more of what you need to know, and less of what you don't.

Packt is a modern, yet unique publishing company, which focuses on producing quality, cutting-edge books for communities of developers, administrators, and newbies alike. For more information, please visit our website: www.packtpub.com.

About Packt Open Source

In 2010, Packt launched two new brands, Packt Open Source and Packt Enterprise, in order to continue its focus on specialization. This book is part of the Packt Open Source brand, home to books published on software built around Open Source licences, and offering information to anybody from advanced developers to budding web designers. The Open Source brand also runs Packt's Open Source Royalty Scheme, by which Packt gives a royalty to each Open Source project about whose software a book is sold.

Writing for Packt

We welcome all inquiries from people who are interested in authoring. Book proposals should be sent to author@packtpub.com. If your book idea is still at an early stage and you would like to discuss it first before writing a formal book proposal, contact us; one of our commissioning editors will get in touch with you.

We're not just looking for published authors; if you have strong technical skills but no writing experience, our experienced editors can help you develop a writing career, or simply get some additional reward for your expertise.

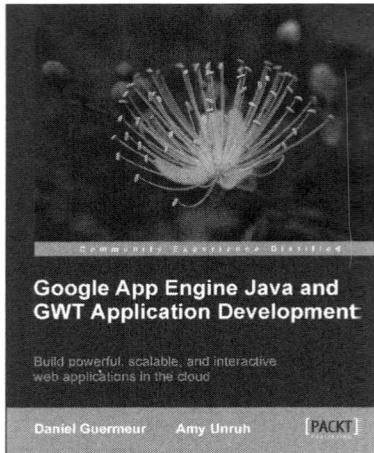

Google App Engine Java and GWT Application Development

ISBN: 978-1-84969-044-7   Paperback: 480 pages

Build powerful, scalable, and interactive web applications in the cloud

1. Comprehensive coverage of building scalable, modular, and maintainable applications with GWT and GAE using Java

2. Leverage the Google App Engine services and enhance your app functionality and performance

3. Integrate your application with Google Accounts, Facebook, and Twitter

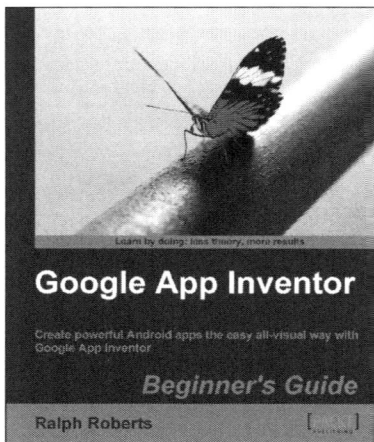

Google App Engine Java and
GWT Application Development

Build powerful, scalable, and interactive
web applications in the cloud

Daniel Guermeur   Amy Unruh   [PACKT]

Google App Inventor

ISBN: 978-1-84969-212-0   Paperback: 356 pages

Create powerful Android apps the easy all-visual way with Google App Inventor

1. All the basics of App Inventor in plain English with lots of illustrations

2. Learn how apps get created with lots of simple, fun examples

3. By an author with over 100 books, who keeps it entertaining, informative, and memorable. You'll be inventing apps from the first day.

Google App Inventor

Create powerful Android apps the easy all-visual way with
Google App Inventor

Beginner's Guide

Ralph Roberts   [PACKT]

Please check **www.PacktPub.com** for information on our titles

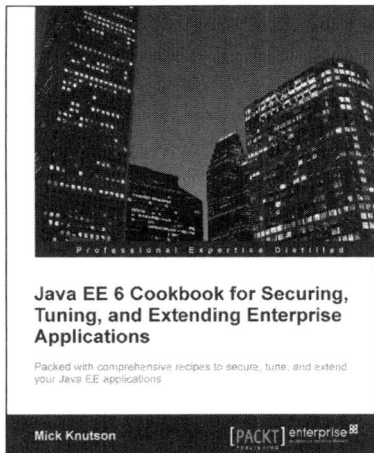

Java EE 6 Cookbook for Securing, Tuning, and Extending Enterprise Applications

ISBN: 978-1-84968-316-6   Paperback: 356 pages

Packed with comprehensive recipes to secure, tune, and extend your Java EE applications

1. Secure your Java applications using Java EE built-in features as well as the well-known Spring Security framework

2. Utilize related recipes for testing various Java EE technologies including JPA, EJB, JSF, and Web services

3. Explore various ways to extend a Java EE environment with the use of additional dynamic languages as well as frameworks

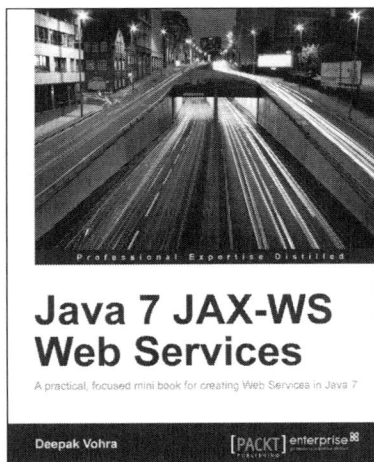

Java EE 6 Cookbook for Securing, Tuning, and Extending Enterprise Applications

Packed with comprehensive recipes to secure, tune, and extend your Java EE applications

Mick Knutson   [PACKT] enterprise⊞

Java 7 JAX-WS Web Services

ISBN: 978-1-84968-720-1   Paperback: 64 pages

A practical, focused mini book for creating Web Services in Java 7

1. Develop Java 7 JAX-WS web services using the NetBeans IDE and Oracle GlassFish server

2. End-to-end application which makes use of the new clientjar option in JAX-WS wsimport tool

3. Packed with ample screenshots and practical instructions

Java 7 JAX-WS Web Services

A practical, focused mini book for creating Web Services in Java 7

Deepak Vohra   [PACKT] enterprise⊞

Please check **www.PacktPub.com** for information on our titles

Printed in Great Britain
by Amazon